STAYING FOCUSED ON GOALS AND PRIORITIES

DUKE CORPORATE EDUCATION

STAYING FOCUSED ON GOALS AND PRIORITIES

Blair Sheppard • Michael Canning
Marla Tuchinsky • Cindy Campbell

President, Dearborn Publishing: Roy Lipner
Vice President and Publisher: Cynthia A. Zigmund
Acquisitions Editor: Jon Malysiak
Senior Project Editor: Trey Thoelcke
Interior Design: Lucy Jenkins
Cover Design: Design Solutions
Typesetting: Elizabeth Pitts

Published by Dearborn Trade Publishing
A Kaplan Professional Company

Printed in the United States of America

06 07 08 10 9 8 7 6 5 4 3 2 1

Library of Congress Cataloging-in-Publication Data

Staying focused on goals and priorities / Duke Corporate Education.
    p. cm.—(Leading from the center)
    Includes bibliographical references and index.
    ISBN 1-4195-1509-8
  1. Leadership. 2. Goal setting in personnel management. I. Duke Corporate Education. II. Series.
  HD57.7.S725 2005
  658.4'092—dc22

                                      2005012557

CONTENTS

ACKNOWLEDGMENTS

First and foremost, we want to thank our clients and the many program participants around the globe. We begin our work by listening to our clients and gaining an understanding of their business challenges. Working with talented clients and actively engaging in their challenges across a range of industries and geographies has afforded us the opportunity to learn and develop an informed point of view on these topics. We thank our clients for trusting in our approach and making us part of their team.

We are also fortunate to have an extensive network of faculty, coaches, facilitators, and partners who believe in our mission and have opted to join in our adventure. Together, we have delivered programs in 37 different countries since Duke Corporate Education (Duke CE) formed in July 2000. We absolutely could not have accomplished what we have and learned what we did without them.

Many thanks to the Dearborn team, who continue to provide valuable feedback and guide us each step of the way. Their assistance and patience is much appreciated.

We were lucky to have the writing and editing assistance of Maureen McGuire Lewis, who assisted with some of the stories and examples that appear here. Her teaching and management experience provided useful insight into the management challenges we describe.

Ryan Stevens worked with us to capture our thoughts and ideas and turn them into the figures included within these pages, often working with vague instructions, such as "It should feel like 'this.'" He did a wonderful job.

Without a doubt the busiest person at Duke CE, our CEO Blair Sheppard, was instrumental to this effort. He supported the initiative from the outset and, more importantly, always made time to review our output and guide our thinking. His assistance is without measure. We could not have done it without him.

We've drawn upon the insights, experiences, and expertise from numerous colleagues here at Duke CE. We hope that the content of this book stimulates your thinking and improves your ability to stay focused on the goals and objectives you want to achieve.

The *Staying Focused on Goals and Priorities* book team: Michael Canning, Marla Tuchinsky, and Cindy Campbell.

In the past 30 years, they have been repeatedly laid off, outsourced, replaced by information technology (IT) applications, and insulted with such derogatory names as "the cement layer." Their bosses accused them of distorting and disrupting communication in their organizations, and their subordinates accused them of thwarting the subordinates' autonomy and empowerment. Who are "they"? Middle managers, those managing in the middle of the organization.

The notion of the middle of an organization has traditionally conjured up a vertical image depicting managers in the middle of a hierarchy. This image carries with it an arcane perception of those managers as gatekeepers and blockages—controlling and slowing down the natural flow of information or resources up or down. It appears to be simple and linear. Given these images, you might think that middle managers are villainous evildoers who sabotage companies or obstructionist bureaucrats who stand in the way of real work getting done. However, the reality is just the opposite. When performed well, the middle manager role is critical in organizations.

Although over the past several decades the value and stature of middle managers has seen both high and low points, we at Duke Corporate Education believe that managing in the middle of the organization has always been both critically important and personally demanding. As one would expect, the essence of the role—the required mind-set and skill set—has continued to change over time. The need to update both of these dimensions is driven by periodic shifts in such underlying forces as marketplace dynamics, technology, organizational structure, and employee expectations. Now and then, these forces converge to create an inflection point that produces a significant change in how organizations are governed, and what role their managers play.

In the *Leading from the Center* series, we examine some of these primary causes that are shaping what it means to successfully lead from the center in the modern organization. We outline the emerging imperative for middle management in an organization as well as the mind-set, knowledge, and skills required to successfully navigate through the most prevalent challenges that lie ahead.

THE NEW CENTER

There are four powerful and pervasive trends affecting the role that managers in the center of an organization are being asked to assume. These trends—information technology, industry convergence, globalization, and regulations—connect directly to the challenges these managers are facing.

Compared to 20 or 30 years ago, *information technology* has escalated the amount, speed, and availability of data to the point that it has changed the way we work and live. Access to information has shifted more power to our customers and suppliers. They not only have more information, but are directly involved in and interacting with the various processes along the value chain. On a personal level, we now find ourselves connected to other people all the time—cell phones, pagers, Blackberries, and PDAs all reinforce the 24/7 culture. The transition from workweek to weekend and back is less distinct. These micro-transitions happen all day, every day because many of us remain connected all the time.

Industries previously seen as separate are now seeing multiple points of *convergence.* Think about how digital technology has led to a convergence of sound, image, text, computing, and communications. Longstanding industry boundaries and parameters are gone (e.g., cable television companies are in the phone business, electronics companies sell music), and along with them, the basis and nature of competition. The boundaries are blurred. It's clear that new possibilities, opportunities, and directions exist, but it isn't always clear what managers should do. Managers will have to be prepared to adapt; their role is to observe, learn from experience, and set direction dynamically. Layered on top of this is the need to manage a more complex set of relationships—cooperating on Monday, competing on Tuesday, and partnering on Wednesday.

Globalization means that assets are now distributed and configured around the world to serve customers and gain competitive advantage. Even companies that consider themselves local interact with global organizations. There is more reliance on fast-developing regional centers of expertise. For example, computer programming in India and manufacturing in China. This means that middle managers are interacting with and coordinating the efforts of people who live in different cultures, and may be awake while their managers are asleep. The notion of a workday has changed as work straddles time zones. Correspondingly, the nature of leading has changed as partnering with vendors and working in virtual teams across regions becomes more common.

The first three forces are causing shifts in the fourth—the *regulatory environment.*

Many industries are experiencing more regulation, while a few others are experiencing less. In some arenas now experiencing more regulation, there is also a drive for more accountability. Demand for more accountability leads to a greater desire to clarify boundaries and roles. Yet there is more ambiguity as to what the rules are and how best to operationalize them. Consider how, in the wake of Sarbanes-Oxley legislation, U.S. companies and accountants continue to sort through the new requirements, while rail companies in Britain are negotiating which company is responsible for maintaining what stretch of tracks. Middle managers sit where regulations get implemented, and are a critical force in shaping how companies respond to the shifts in the environment.

An additional force adding to the managerial complexity is the shifting demographics in the workforce. An aging workforce is having two effects. One is a loss of knowledge and talent as a large number of Baby Boomers enter retirement. The other is that people are living longer and want to stay active both physically and economically; so, we are also seeing an increased number of older people returning to the workforce, even if in a different field. It will be more common in the future to be managing three different generations of workers, each with its own beliefs, experiences, aspirations and views of work. Both trends impact the complexity of the manager's challenges.

The connection between strategy development and strategy execution becomes tighter every day; so, people in the middle of the hierarchy who understand the strategy but live near the action become more pivotal and important. It will be up to them to simultaneously manage the communication, coordination, and connections required to translate the strategic direction into action and feedback— what's working and what's not—and continue to dynamically shape the strategy.

In addition to communicating and coordinating more actively up and down in your organization, many of you no doubt now find yourselves navigating and managing in a matrix, and as part of one or more networks. Your formal authority may still exist vertically, but your real power to achieve results stems from your ability to work across all levels and boundaries. From the center, you act as an integrator, sense maker, and catalyst. As depicted in Figure I.1, you are now in the heart of the action, and central to the future success of the organization. Leading from the center produces new and interesting challenges, tensions, and opportunities.

IF YOU ARE LEADING FROM THE CENTER

If you are a manager in the center today, you have many hats to wear, more balls to juggle, and fewer certainties in your work environment. You have to be adaptive yet provide continuity in your leadership. You need to simultaneously translate strategy, influence and collaborate, lead teams, coach and motivate your people, support innovation, and own the systems and processes—all in the service of getting results. Those in the center need more courage than ever. They are the conscience of their organizations, carrying forth the values. At the same time they build today's and tomorrow's business success.

FIGURE I.I In the Center of the Action

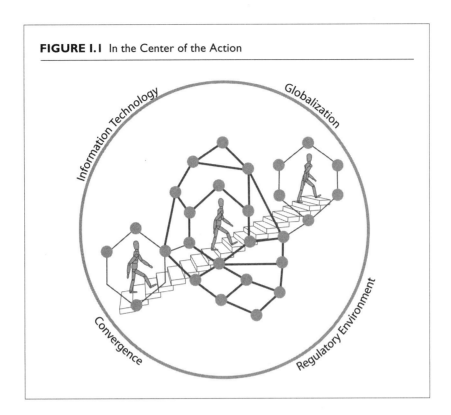

Strategy Translator

As a strategy translator, you must first understand the corporate strategy and determine what parts of it your group can best support. Next, you must translate it into an action plan for your group, making sure it aligns well with the overall strategy. You'll need to consider which projects are essential stepping stones and which are needed in their own right, and establish some priorities or guiding goals. You must then communicate the details of the plan and priorities, and create momentum around them. As your team implements, you'll need to involve not only your people but to also collaborate and coordinate with others, including peers, customers, and other units. Instead of directing a one-way downward flow of information, you must translate upward as well and act as a conduit for strategic feedback to the executives above.

Influencer and Collaborator for Results

Middle managers must learn how to make things happen by influencing, integrating, and collaborating across the boundaries of the organization. As a manager, instead of focusing exclusively on your piece, you have to look outside of your own group to develop a network of supporting relationships. Rather than issuing commands and asserting power based on your position, you have to use other tactics to gain agreement and make things happen.

Leader of Teams

Teams have become a one-size-fits-all solution for organizing work in today's economy—virtual teams, project teams, product teams, and function-specific teams—and can be either the blessing or the bane of many companies. Your role as a manager includes understanding the challenges of teams and facilitating their development so that they can be effective more quickly. You have to align the team's energy and talents in a way that will deliver the desired results. You are responsible for creating an environment that will help this group of people work well together to achieve today's objectives and to develop the skills needed to take on future goals.

Coach and Motivator

While many organizations are well positioned to execute their strategies in yesterday's environment, they are moderately able to meet their current needs and often they are not thinking about how to position themselves for the future. From the center of the organization, middle managers assume much of the responsibility for their people. They create an environment to attract and retain good employees, coach them to do their current jobs better, and bear primary responsibility for developing others. As a manager, you must figure out how to build the next level of capability, protect existing people, connect their aspirations to opportunities for development, and make work more enjoyable. You need to provide regular feedback—both positive and redirecting—and build strong relationships with those who surround you. If done well, your departments will be more efficient and your employees will be better equipped to become leaders in their own right.

Intrapreneur/Innovator

Enabling and supporting an innovative approach within your company will foster the strategic direction of the future. To effectively sponsor innovation, you need to create the context for your people, foster a climate that supports innovative efforts, and actively sponsor the ideas of the future. You have to *be* innovative and *lead* the innovative efforts of others. Innovation is most often associated with new-product development, but innovative approaches also are needed in developing new services or solving internal system and process problems. As a manager, you use their influence and relationships to find the root cause of problems, and the resources to make change happen.

Owner of Systems and Processes

Managers need to understand that part of their role is to take ownership for architecting new systems and processes. You have to shift your thinking from living within existing systems and processes to making sure that those systems and processes work well: Do the systems and processes support or get in the way of progress? One of the mistakes we have made in the past is to not hold managers accountable for their role in architecting the next generation of systems and processes. As a manager, you must perform harsh audits of existing systems, and understand when to tear down what may have been left in place from a past strategy. You need to assess what is no longer relevant and/or is no longer working. Part of your responsibility is to think about and decide whether to reengineer or remove existing systems.

CAN YOU DO IT ALL?

Our lives seem to grow even busier, and our time and focus shorter. As the challenges at work mount, so do your responsibilities and aspirations in the other domains of your life—family, friends, community, physical health, finances. Given the range of things you are called on to deal with every day, with limited attention and resources, you may occasionally feel as if you are less effective across all areas your life. If this is true for you, chances are your people are feeling the same pressures.

What can you do to help yourself and others be more focused and get the results that you envision, even when it feels as if you are often in the midst of chaos? As you have probably already discovered, there is no silver bullet or single answer. Being more effective in this new, complex world requires a shift in thinking and action, and some new tools and techniques. You need to create a lifestyle that supports your aims, and the shifts in them. This book will guide you through a process that couples self-insight (understanding your values, your unique talents, and what you want to create in your life) with application (using routines, techniques, and tools to keep you on track and reinforce your efforts along the way).

The goal is to create a life where you are more effective at achieving the results you want as an individual and as a leader of others.

THE CHALLENGE OF STAYING FOCUSED

IN THE MIDST OF CHAOS

Miranda bolted upright in bed. She'd forgotten to silence her cell phone, which was singing its familiar tune. "Who would be calling now?" she thought to herself. She slid out of bed and rushed to the kitchen, closing the hall door so the sleeping household wouldn't hear her. She flipped the phone open and listened to a loud voice say they had found her laptop in the X-ray room at County Hospital. "Thanks so much," Miranda replied, and she asked them to hold it at Security until she could pick it up in the morning on the way to the airport. Hanging up, she realized she had not even missed it.

Earlier that day her son Jake had fallen at school, fracturing his right thumb and prompting her mad dash to the school and then to the emergency room. When the school called, Miranda had been in the middle of preparing for a big presentation for the next day. Once at the hospital, she had juggled comforting Jake, talking to doctors, and slipping outside to call and touch base with her staff (no phones allowed in the ER!), who had continued the preparations without her. She'd tried not to answer her cell phone unless she knew it was her staff calling, and now had a full voice mailbox of messages, most of them claiming to be about something urgent.

Miranda sat down and gave a sigh of relief that her computer was at least safe. Thankfully, she wouldn't have to explain how *that* happened back at her office. But wait . . . , she groaned, as she realized she had no idea what airline she was flying on in the morning. That information was on her laptop's online calendar, and her PDA also was in the case with the laptop. Her assistant would have the information, but that would require either a late night or early morning call, neither of which Miranda wanted to make. This meant she would have to leave before 6:00 AM to retrieve the laptop so she could find out on which airline her flight was booked. That, in turn, meant she wouldn't see Jake or her other kids before she left. Her husband would have to handle all the morning preparations for school, dealing with Jake's pain and confusion about his hand cast, and she knew that his work schedule was as hectic as usual.

Miranda had also assured her assistant that she would be sending specific instructions on what questions to ask the morning's client. In the past two days, there had been no time to spend with her staff; it had been "crisis mode" with everyone running around trying to meet another deadline. She had tried to piece together something while at the hospital, but it wasn't nearly complete, and she felt guilty that she hadn't delivered for the client or her team. She worried that her afternoon away from the office meant even more "crisis" e-mails were piling up in her inbox. She had also planned to work on the financial figures that were due to accounting in two days and realized her team's projections would be late yet again.

Miranda decided she'd drive out to the hospital immediately, even though it was after midnight, to pick up her laptop and find out which airline she'd be taking, and more importantly, what time she needed to be at the airport. In the morning she'd send her instructions and questions, say goodbye to the kids, help her husband, and pack her bag. "Why is everything so complicated, so demanding, so draining?" she thought as she scribbled a note to her husband and threw on some clothes and shoes. As she started her car, Miranda hoped that she wouldn't be completely exhausted by the time she was scheduled to give her presentation in the afternoon.

Miranda is not alone. Perhaps you have entertained friends and coworkers with your own version of a "Miranda" story—if you could laugh about the situation afterwards. Although days that require a trip to the emergency room are hopefully not the norm, staying focused, feeling effective in all the areas of our lives, and achieving the results we want are a daily struggle. At the end of a typical day, how often do you find yourself questioning what you actually accomplished that day? How often do you question whether the most important tasks or the people and things you value the most are getting the attention they deserve? How often do you wonder how things got so far out of alignment, and how to regain your equilibrium and focus? How often do you observe members of your team struggling in the same way?

HOW DID THIS CHAOS HAPPEN?

The Boundaries Are Blurring

The technologies that have enabled us to do more have also redefined *when* we can do it. The boundaries between our life domains continue to blur as we try to integrate all the existing pieces of our lives, and to fit even more pieces in. We used to have stronger divisions between our life domains—work, family, leisure, community— and the time and attention we gave to each. The workday for the majority of people occurred between 8 AM and 5 PM, five days a week, and we recognized the "lunch hour." Our evenings and weekends were set aside for family, friends, hobbies, and community or spiritual activities. Now, we bring work home with us, our kids send instant messages to our cell phone during the school day (from their own cell phone no less!), our accountant sends an e-mail to our work account, and we plan our church charity bazaar on our laptop while watching the kids' soccer game. Technology has both removed the restrictions that we used to have, and along with that, the boundaries that helped give structure to the pieces of our lives.

Rather than the larger, clearer transitions we enjoyed in the past, today we are constantly making micro-transitions between the different domains in our lives. Many people in our personal network also do business with us. Being more connected has added to the complexity and interdependence between all the parts and pieces. It's becoming harder to separate family from work from community from ourselves. We are all becoming more accessible to more people more of the time.

A Manager's Role Is Changing

Managers' roles are changing. In the past, as you ascended in the hierarchy, you typically shifted away from being a "doer," someone who did the work and accomplished results directly. Doing, for a manager, was then to get work done indirectly through others. A by-product of the dynamic world we operate in is that it has become more important for all of us to stay connected to the customers, competition, and environment in which we do business.

For example, a vice president in a large investment bank may retain responsibility for and provide service to some key accounts. In the past such a vice president would have stopped seeing customers at this level of responsibility; today he or she still meets with them, offers advice, and handles most aspects of their accounts. More and more, managers remain "doers" and are also responsible for managing. The more dynamic the knowledge and environment, the more important it is to stay directly connected to keep your knowledge current and credibility high.

The Bar Really Is Getting Higher

The expectations are being raised both in terms of the performance levels that our employers expect of us and the demands we in turn impose on ourselves to try and achieve those levels.

In an attempt to do it all, we try to find ways to fit more in and reach more people—taking our laptops on vacation so we can check e-mail, listening to voice mail during an intermission in the school play, talking with clients while driving to the next commitment. With overlapping demands, shorter deadlines, fewer breaks and reflection points, and more to remember, people are realizing more and more that they cannot do it all. They may wake up feeling overwhelmed, or they can't remember why they loved their job, or they have a sinking feeling that they aren't doing anything as well as they would like. They may feel ineffective, dissatisfied, and distracted.

With all this technology, we rationalize that it *should* be easier and we *should* be able to do more. Often, one of the first things we try is to replace the technology we have with new technology: One that goes faster or farther or combines five devices into one. If we can talk, read e-mail, take photos, listen to music, download documents, and make appointments all with one device, then surely we can get more done and be more effective.

The very technologies that were designed to make us more connected and effective—cell phones, pagers, PDAs, e-mail—may actually end up making us feel disconnected and ineffective. Technology has become both a promise and a curse. There is the promise of greater connectivity and efficiency, but also the curse of higher expectations and demands. The promise of "anytime, anywhere" has turned into the curse of "all the time, everywhere."

These Fundamental Changes (Increased Technology, Blurred Boundaries, Changing Roles, and a Bar That Continues to Rise) Aren't Going Away

Some try to use old tools and an old mind-set to combat these changes, gaining leverage by working harder and longer. For some of us, finding ways to fit more in can be like an addiction. We can actually thrive on the adrenaline and may boast to others about needing only four hours of sleep; but eventually, the energy runs out, and we find ourselves in overload. We lose sight of what is really important to us, make decisions that we later regret, and feel as if we aren't doing *anything* well. Loehr and Schwartz (2003) write that the Japanese report around 10,000 cases a year of "karoshi," or "death from overwork." Some of the most common factors associated with karoshi cases are long hours without rest, working well into the evenings, not taking holidays or breaks, and the pressure of physical and mental stress. Sound familiar?

Trying to fit more and more into our schedules has an impact across all the domains of our lives. It spills over and has detrimental effects on those around us, too. Studies show that our kids are as overscheduled as we are, going from practice to clubs to events with no time in between. Some parents say that they view this hectic lifestyle as necessary "training" for the adult lives their kids will one day find themselves in. More of our pets are overweight and neurotic, and they are often left home alone or in kennels. Our civic activities have declined; we are less engaged in the issues confronting our schools, environment, or community. We are experiencing more physical and mental health problems—high blood pressure, diabetes, obesity, anxiety, and depression. (De Graaf, 2003)

In this book, we make the case for finding equilibrium in your life by using new tools and a new mind-set. Getting focused, improving your effectiveness, and achieving results start with creating a foundation of equilibrium that works for you and by identifying those things that will help you hold a steady course—your bearings if you will—in the midst of chaos as you quickly transition from one life domain to another. You might be thinking, "Oh, this is a book about work-life balance, or perhaps time management. I get it." Not quite. To be clear, we are talking about finding your equilibrium and staying focused. We are not talking about equally balancing all the pieces nor are we advocating that the answer is simply to manage time more efficiently.

"O.K., here I am in the fourth grade, but is that really
what I want to be doing with my life?"

The phrase "work-life balance" implies there are only two aspects to your life—work and life other than work—and that they are mutually exclusive. In reality, work is a significant part of life for many people, but it is neither separate nor performed in isolation from the other elements. Further, the phrase implies that "work" and "life" should be given equal weight (time, energy, attention, etc.), where achieving perfect equality is the desired and desirable goal. This notion is naive.

In contrast, a foundation of equilibrium isn't about two elements being equal, and it's not about fitting everything in by just managing your time more efficiently as some would have us believe. *It is about managing your energy—deciding what's important and staying focused on those things.* It's about making conscious choices and building a support system to help you, rather than simply weathering whatever comes along and hoping for the best. It's about staying connected to those who matter to you and engaging them. It's about making choices when opportunities present themselves and navigating the myriad micro-transitions we face each day in managing our interests, relationships, desires, time, and resources.

There are many equilibrium points possible, depending on where you are in your life, your current priorities, and how others around you react. Making conscious choices and being deliberately unequal are healthy aims. How do you stay focused and true? You need a new mind-set that *focuses on life as a series of intervals* instead of one long marathon. Next, you need to *build and keep strong relationships;* there are other characters in those chapters or intervals and they are the glue and enablers that help you "keep it together." Finally, in this dynamic environment, you need to *be clear what you value and why,* because this will help set your focus and your choices and, ultimately, make you more effective.

APPROACH LIFE AS A SERIES OF INTERVALS

There are some predictable and natural sequences to our lives, like books with similar chapter headings. We're born and spend childhood learning about the world and society; we go to school; we find an occupation; we have "big birthdays"; we get promotions; we retire or change jobs or both; we lose people who are close to us; we go to weddings, maybe our own; we hear of divorces, maybe our own; we take an important trip; we move; we spend holidays with family or friends. Although the content of our individual chapters may be wildly different, the broad developmental pattern is similar.

As we transition between major chapters of our lives, it's important to reflect, gain insight into ourselves and our situation, make adjustments, and confirm what's really most important to us, because in no chapter can you do it all. We need to see life holistically and be planful, and also understand that our priorities shift as we develop and move through different chapters.

While this is critical, it's equally important in today's hectic, dynamic world to remain agile and adaptable in the execution of each chapter. We plan for chapters but live our lives in smaller intervals—hours, days, weeks. Our ability to identify and make these many microtransitions as we move from one task to the next, one person to the next, and one day to the next, is critical. To succeed today, companies must understand their environment, develop a strategy, and then be adaptable and capable of seizing the emergent opportunities. Like companies, we need to do the same as individuals. Dynamic times require that we get comfortable with these apparent paradoxes—planning the chapters, but living out each page adaptively. The ability to reassess and orient ourselves between chapters and reassess and make choices and adjustments regularly as we live them out is the way to get the best possible results and to live our best lives.

Get Very Efficient at the Phase You're In

Don't treat one phase or interval as merely a temporary stepping stone to something more important. Instead of focusing too far ahead, focus on the present, then treat it as a foundation block for the next phase. Do this phase well and use it to build your connections with others and to explore your talents.

There was a time when Olympic athletes trained for a solid six hours or more every day. They believed that the more time they could spend on their sport, the stronger, faster, and better they would become. Now, though, such elite athletes have moved away from long training sessions. Instead of lifting weights for three hours, five times a week, they have found that shorter, more varied workouts have just as much, if not more, benefit. As Groppel and Andelman (2000) note, athletes who work their bodies in a 60- or 90-minute interval, take a break, and then train again, are more efficient and more effective than those who go for longer sessions. It seems that we as humans are designed for short sprints or middle distance, not supermarathons.

Reflect and Adapt More Frequently and More Purposefully

The standard advice has often been to step back, reflect, and set a clear plan. We agree that reflection is an important activity, but would argue that it's not something you do only when you're under pressure or feel out of alignment. You need to continually take time to reflect, discuss things with others, and make shifts in your goals, approach, or routines. Make minor adjustments all the time, and larger changes when appropriate. Smaller chunks of time are easier to understand and to do something with. With more frequent periods of reflection we can accomplish the following:

- *Take advantage of opportunities as they occur.* Things happen quickly, and you may not have this particular option again. As the old saying goes, "Be ready when opportunity knocks."
- *Make more frequent adjustments and stay in alignment.* You don't need to wait until it's become a "problem." Minor adjustments are less disruptive. When you drive, you are constantly making small adjustments to steer the car. Don't wait until you've swerved completely off the road before correcting your course.
- *Make larger changes if problems have developed.*

U.S. Air Force Colonel John. R. Boyd knew how to train people to succeed in dynamic situations. Based on his experience training military flyers, Boyd was a strong advocate for reflecting on the changing circumstances and making regular adjustments. He spent years studying how he and other military flyers understood their changing situation and gained advantage over an adversary. He summarized his strategy as OODA—Observe, Orient, Decide, and Act. (See Figure 1.1) Orientation is how people interpret a situation based on their perspective, shaped by both past and present. In a dynamic situation, those who can rapidly observe and assess a situation, find a new twist, reorient themselves, adapt and make good decisions, will have the advantage. As a manager, you too need to take time to reorient yourself as the situation changes; reflect before acting.

Recognize and Reset When Chapters Change

People get accustomed to small adjustments; however, one of the most common mistakes that they make is failing to understand and adapt when larger change happens. When you move from one chapter to another—graduate from college, get your first job, become a parent, assume more responsibility or a different management role—there are corresponding shifts in your vision of where you want to be, what you value most in that chapter, and the talents and skills you need to succeed. Too often, people blithely continue in the same routines and behaviors and quickly get out of alignment. Their mind-set may still be that of a graduate student when they are in fact now an employee or a manager. The more out of step we are, the harder it is to stay focused or be effective. We may lose touch with people whom we care about, we may forget to be good coaches and mentors, and we may not feel quite right about who we have become. The game changed and we didn't change with it. Occasionally our system is out of equilibrium, and we need to reflect and reset in order to steady ourselves.

FIGURE 1.1 The OODA Loop

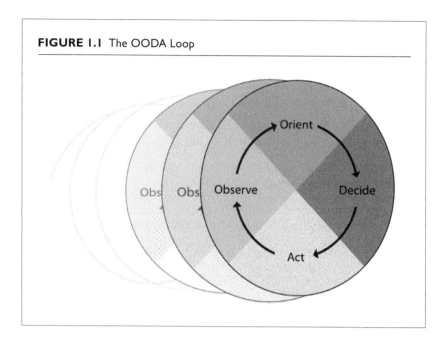

KNOW WHAT YOU VALUE AND BELIEVE IN

Life is serendipitous. We rarely know what opportunities will present themselves to us, how we and those close to us will respond, and how to best navigate these opportunities. The unpredictability we experience is exactly what can make our life chapters interesting.

This unpredictability also can be a source of anxiety for some. They build a solid plan, spanning several years, and methodically set out to achieve it. If this is truly a dream come true, the result can be amazing. If the dreams change, though, or the reality isn't as good as expected, they may find themselves regretting their choices, regretting not having seized some of the serendipitous prospects that arose over the years. Not a happy ending, is it? So, how do we keep some order in our lives, yet still be able to follow unexpected paths when they appear to us? Consider the following:

- *Be clear about what you value and what you believe in.* This gives you a standard to judge each opportunity and understand if or

how it will fit. It provides a stable core that you can center yourself around as situations change around you.

- *Be adaptable.* Many events don't unfold as we expect. Learn to
  say, "That's okay," and figure out how to make the most of
  what does happen. Connect goals and priorities to your values
  and emotions. Be open to getting to the same place another
  way, or getting to an entirely new place.
- *Imagine several steps out.* Connect each opportunity to what you
  care about and what offers most leverage for the future. Imagine how an opportunity will affect those you care about, or
  what changes it will force on them (both positive and negative).

ENGAGE OTHERS

You Can't Do It Alone

We don't go through our life chapters or intervals in isolation. In
every life chapter, you are interdependent with other people—parents, spouses, coworkers, clients, bosses, friends, and so on. When
we get overwhelmed, there's a tendency to put our relationships on
hold while we concentrate more on whatever life domain is demanding our attention at that point in time. We don't take as much time
with people, we reach out less, and we make one-sided plans. Although a natural reaction, it is the opposite of what you *should* do.
You should ask for help or advice, make a point of continuing your
social life and see whom you might engage with.

Understand the Value of Reciprocity

Neither should we reach out to others only in the interest of what
they can do for us. There are more benefits to forming relationships
than "What's in it for me?" You need to understand how to help others, and how to let others help you. You need to make investments in
relationships, and leverage the places where you can assist one an-

other. Help each other, perhaps without receiving any immediate benefits, but believing that benefits eventually find their way back to the original giver.

What drives our sense of reciprocity? Scientists at the Yerkes National Primate Research Center in Atlanta conducted experiments in which capuchin monkeys were taught to reach a cup of food on a tray by pulling on a bar attached to the tray. The tray was too heavy for a single monkey, thus giving them a reason to work together. During one experiment, the monkeys successfully brought a tray within reach, but one monkey, Sammy, was in such a hurry to reach her food reward that she released the bar and grabbed her cup before the other monkey had a chance to retrieve hers. As might our experience with humans predict, Bias, the monkey who didn't get food, threw a screaming temper tantrum; that is, until Sammy returned to pull the bar again and help her to retrieve her food, too. Clearly it wasn't for Sammy's own benefit, because she had already eaten. Her response, researchers believe, comes close to human economic transactions—it shows cooperation, communication, and maybe even a sense of obligation. (De Waal, 2003)

Leverage Our Combined Talents, Gifts, and Skills

As managers, parents, mentors, and friends, we build relationships with others. We learn from them, and offer coaching to them. We focus on what we each are good at, and then play to our strengths. Similarly, we establish relationships with professionals who offer customized or personalized support: personal trainers, coaches or tutors, personal shoppers, personal chefs, wedding planners, financial advisors, and so on. Instead of sorting through general information step-by-step, from A to B to C, and then tailoring it ourselves, we can hire experts who can jump right in at step G, because step G is really where we need to be. We can be more efficient and get better service and results by recognizing what we are *not* good at and trusting others who are better at those things to do it for us. Think of it as requiring self-management to trust someone else and let go, and relationship management to know whom to share with, entrust, or hand off to, allowing them to take some of the load.

WHAT'S COMING

We'll revisit each of these guiding ideas throughout the book. In the following chapters, we look at specific ways to help you find equilibrium points that will work to help you stay focused. By doing so, you will in turn learn how to be more effective as an individual and as a leader, and also how to help others achieve that same level of focus.

We begin with reflection and self-insight; that is, where you are, what you're doing, and what you want to pursue. Some aspects are time specific, such as what's important to you right now, and some aspects reflect your core values. First, we help you define where you want to be or your vision of the future by considering the importance of each of your life domains. The goal is to envision success in this chapter of your life and in future chapters as well. Which items have a higher priority for you at this chapter? We'll explore what you value, and when put to the test, how your choices are reinforcing those values. Finally, we'll consider what talents, skills, gifts, and knowledge you possess, or those things that you do best. This is what you bring to the table in your relationships and collaborations with others.

We then focus on techniques to reinforce and support your efforts. Setting specific goals, calibrating how you're doing, measuring progress, and celebrating success will help you achieve the results you envision. We'll review the value of routines and how they can support your efforts when used effectively. Finally, we'll consider your role as a leader—how you can both realize the benefits of these techniques as well as model them for others. We end by offering advice on transitioning and resetting your focus.

Remember, this is not about a "once in ten years" checkup; it's about creating a *lifestyle* that works for you and enables you to achieve the results you want as an individual and as a leader of others.

FIGURE 1.2 Getting Focused

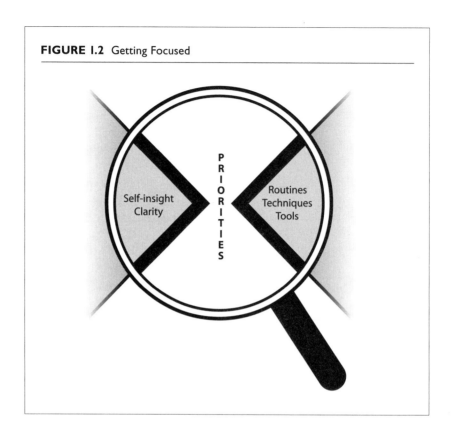

CHAPTER TWO

FINDING YOUR EQUILIBRIUM

IN THIS CHAPTER

Where Do You Want to Go? ■ What Do You Value? ■
What Will Help You Get There? ■ Be Reflective and Make
Connections ■ Help Others with the Process

We need to gain insight into our visions, our values, and our talents in order to find the equilibrium that will help us achieve the results we want.

- *Vision.* Our aspirations, or where we want to go
- *Values.* Our core beliefs, or what is most important to us
- *Talents.* Our unique capabilities and gifts that will help get us there

WHERE DO YOU WANT TO GO?

"What would you like to accomplish in your current position?" "Where do you see yourself in five years or ten years?" "What are your aspirations?" "Do you have a plan for achieving your goals?" You've probably responded to variations of these questions in your career.

Chances are you've also posed some of these questions to others during interviews or performance evaluations. For many, these are the types of questions that we dread—especially if you, in fact, don't have a clear vision of where you want to go or a plan for getting there.

Consider your own responses and the responses of others that you've heard over time. Are they predictable? Maybe you approached these questions with a heartfelt and thoughtful answer; or maybe you responded to them with what you thought was the "right" answer based on who was asking. Chances are you focused on the immediate particulars of your job, and not on integrating all the parts and pieces of your life. Even though many of our life domains are blurred and inseparable, some of us still tend to think that we can neatly separate them and have a clear but segmented vision of our future. "This is where I want to be in my career" and "This is where I want to live" and "This is what my family will be like"—we end up with disconnected pieces, not a coherent vision.

Maybe you outlined and followed a clear plan that took you to where you are today. If you did, you are probably the exception. For many of us, our current situation may be simply a matter of chance and circumstance. Many people report that they didn't necessarily select the work field they now find themselves in, strive to the position they now hold, or consciously choose to spend their time and energy on all of the things that are now in their lives. Things just sort of "happened," they reacted, and this is somehow where they ended up. Either something interesting presented itself or they didn't envision something better, so they went along.

As you already know, life is dynamic. Events will happen, paths will change, and boundaries will blur even more. It won't be simple or easy. It won't always go according to plan, nor should it, because that's what keeps life interesting—the plot twists that fill the chapters and scenes. We're *not* talking about following a rigid path; that almost certainly won't work. Equilibrium is about having a vision of the life that you want in this chapter, and maybe some future one, and staying focused on your current path. If you are going to find equilibrium, you need to decide what's really important and develop a personal vision describing elements of your future.

Although the fourth grade was probably a bit too early to begin thinking about long-term financial goals, college majors, or vacation homes, it was a perfect time to think about sports you would like to play, which summer camps offered the things you liked, musical instruments you wanted to learn how to play, or whether you would like to run for class president or treasurer. In other words, be present in the present, and maybe do loose positioning for upcoming chapters.

Have Courage

Real insight and honesty about both where you want to be and where you are today is a simple concept, but one that takes time, space, and courage. It is an exercise of deep self-examination, and first attempts at a personal vision are typically incomplete. You might leave out a significant area of your life. You might immediately filter portions of your vision as impossible to achieve for some reason and not even bother to state them. You may have difficulty completely describing your vision of the future because you really don't know what it is you want. Sometimes what we want is so deep and personal that we haven't admitted it even to ourselves. Sometimes, it's painful to take an honest look at who we are, warts and all.

One approach to thinking about your vision of where you want to be is to begin with a list of the various domains of your life and answer some basic questions about each. Identify all of the possibilities and consider what's important to you. Resist the urge to judge and modify your answers. There are no wrong or right answers, and no one is peeking over your shoulder at your responses. It's okay to say that you want to make enough money to afford gardeners, cooks, chauffeurs, nannies, and personal shoppers. It's also okay to say that you have all this today but what you really want is to have the time to do all these things for yourself. Keep in mind that your answers are a reflection of where you are in your current life's chapter; your answers will change as your situation changes.

Consider each of the familiar life domains found in Figure 2.1. How would you answer these questions today?

FIGURE 2.1 Life Domains

Physical Health	What level of physical health do you want? For example, do you want to be illness-free, physically fit, or participating in competitive athletics? Do existing physical difficulties affect your abilities in other domains?
Spiritual and Emotional Health	What is your life philosophy? What beliefs and traditions are important to you? How comfortable are you with your inner self? How do you approach the world—your mood, general outlook, reactions to life's ups and downs? How robust is your support network?
Work	What type of work do you want to do? What type of environment do you prefer? What effect will you have in your role or profession?
Family and Home	How are your relationships with family members—parents, siblings, and/or children? What romantic relationships do you want? What is your ideal living environment? What mood does your home evoke in you?
Friends and Leisure	How important are friends in your life? How involved do you want to be with one another's day-to-day life? What hobbies or interests do you want to pursue or continue? What will you do for fun and relaxation? How much time, energy, or attention do you want to expend?
Civic/ Community	What type of community do you want to be a part of? What organizations do you want to be a member of or volunteer with? What events or services do you look for?
Financial	How much money do you want or need? Do you want/need to be able to financially support other family members? When do you want to retire and what resources will that require?

Senge, et al. (1994) provide an exercise to expand your understanding of what's important to you. Begin with an initial desire that you have listed in one of your life domains and ask the question, "If I had it, what would it bring me?" For each answer, ask the question again, "And what would *that* bring me?" until you peel away the layers and gain a deeper understanding of what it is you are seeking.

Let's try another exercise. First, imagine that you are now an 85-year-old grandmother or grandfather. You've been telling your grandchildren about your life, and they've heard the story up to the point that you finished reading this book (the age you are now). You are about to continue describing what happened from that point. What events would you like to tell them about? What would you be most proud of? How would you like to characterize your life? If you had to summarize particular accomplishments, behaviors, or feelings around each life domain, what would you note?

Now, let's return our attention to your situation. Looking across the same domains, what is your life like today? How would you like it to be? Which areas are in need of real attention and care at this point? If an area is getting less attention now, do you understand why? It may be simply a result of the chapter of life you are currently in, and that's okay. It's a question of making deliberate choices about your attention. ("You can have it all, just maybe not all at once.") Think about the gap between where you are today and the hypothetical "life" you just looked back on as an 85-year-old. What type of lifestyle changes do you want to make and how will you do it?

WHAT DO YOU VALUE?

What do you most value? What are your core beliefs? Do the choices you make day-to-day align with what you claim to care deeply about? Are they really the choices *you* want to make? Do they support the results you want to get, that is, those things you've described in your vision of where you want to go? When pressed to choose, it should be clear what you value, and whether your choices are true to those values.

How do the choices you *want* to make stand up against the pressures of daily reality? We're reminded of a personal insurance advertising campaign that used the slogan "Life comes at you fast." The television commercial flashes scenes of a variety of events that could happen to you—shopping carts hitting your car in the grocery store parking lot, a strong wind toppling a tree onto the roof of your home, a delivery man tripping over something in your driveway and landing face first on the ground. The message is clear: Things are going to happen, and you need to invest in insurance beforehand, because after it happens is too late. In much the same way, you need to invest in deciding what values and lifestyle vision will drive all the spontaneous choices that you will have to make each day. It may seem straightforward, but in the midst of the daily chaos we find ourselves in (remember Miranda from Chapter 1), without steady equilibrium bearings we can quickly lose focus on goals and objectives.

At Duke CE, we occasionally use an exercise called the *Values Auction* to demonstrate how hard it can be to make these choices. The exercise typically begins with a group of approximately 15 participants. We give all participants a list of bid items that will be auctioned off and instruct them to plan their bid strategy (circle their top five to ten choices, and then have them decide how to allocate an imaginary $1,000 across these priority items). Each item is scarce—only one in the auction—and only the winning bidder gets to have the item in his or her life. Once the bidding begins, as in a real auction, bidders have to make quick decisions. The situation becomes more "real" when participants begin bidding against each other for the same items of value, and they don't always win what they want. How much are they willing to invest in a single item? What other items are they willing to give up in order to secure it? After all, if they spend too much of their money on an early item, they may not have enough left over for other items further down the list. Or they may end up with a variety of things that they find they don't really value. A sampling of items that might appear on the bid list is shown in Figure 2.2. Each person has items he or she values highly and would immediately add to his or her list, but then must choose because $1,000 doesn't go far.

FIGURE 2.2 Sample Values Auction Bid List

- ❏ Being the "go to" person whenever anyone needs an innovative solution.
- ❏ Never having to see a doctor again.
- ❏ Never having to worry about losing your job.
- ❏ Being attractive and stylish for the next 15 years.
- ❏ Being very well known and well respected in your field.
- ❏ Having your word be better than a signed contract.
- ❏ Getting to live in the house of your dreams.
- ❏ Having a warm and loving family.
- ❏ Always keeping your self-respect.
- ❏ Profoundly and positively changing the lives of others through your actions.
- ❏ Never having to worry about money again.
- ❏ Being loyal to your family and friends and having them remain loyal in return.
- ❏ Having a healthy relationship with the love of your life.
- ❏ Experiencing spiritual health and well-being.
- ❏ Living a varied and stimulating life.
- ❏ Working in a challenging and competitive environment.

What do you value most today? Keep in mind that your life will change and what is not as important today may have greater significance at a later point. Never having to see a doctor again may not be something you value highly if you're young and in good health; however, it takes on a different significance if you're older and experiencing increasing health problems. Never having to worry about losing your job has more appeal for those who work in a volatile industry, who have lost jobs previously, or who have an extended family to support.

Ask for Others' Perspectives

You think you're making the right choices and going in the right direction. However, would the people who live or work with you agree with the choices you make and how you spend your time and energy? If asked to predict what choices you would make in the Values Auction, what would they say? Based on your previous history, they may predict a different top ten list.

When you ask for others' input, their answers may surprise you. The messages you intend to send may not be arriving; the choices you have made in the past may not reflect these values. For example, if your intent is to have some family time in the evenings and you leave work early to do so, but then immediately after dinner begin making phone calls and responding to e-mail, your family may not see that you view them as a priority. If you say that one of your priorities is to build a collaborative team environment, but you frequently cancel team meetings when "more important" meetings come up, the message you send may not be what you intended.

As an example, let's take a look at Sebastian, a guy who feels he's at the top of his game. Through many years at his midsized company, Sebastian fell out of the habit of asking for input. There simply was not enough time, and he was always in demand. As Director of Human Resources, each week he received dozens of requests to meet with this group, arrange that interview, or facilitate another meeting. He felt alive, plugged in, and thrived on the continuous activity. People envied his high energy level, although in the past year, as he moved into his 50s, that energy often waned.

His three staff members were competent workers, all with 5 or more years of experience at the company. However, Sebastian was not aware of their growing anger and resentment. For the past 14 months, every three out of four staff meetings were nonproductive. This fact irritated Sebastian, but he rarely thought about the reasons behind it.

If someone had asked each of his three staff members what accounted for the nonproductive meetings, they would have had no trouble attributing reasons. Ariel would have said, "Sebastian likes being in command and control of everything. He rarely delegates anything important to any of us." Antonio would claim, with barely hidden annoyance, "He is chronically late to meetings, 20 to 30 minutes late, and then expects us to act as if that's perfectly normal. No apologies, no excuses. It's galling." Stephen would put it more bluntly: "Sebastian is all about Sebastian, nothing else."

Seek Assistance

You can't do it alone. You've likely discovered that you need to make some changes if you are going to realize your future vision. Who can you count on for support? Many of these items will affect those close to you as well as depend on their support. How much support will you need and from whom? What resources can you call on? What can you do for them in return?

For example, if you have decided that each Wednesday afternoon you will leave work early for a family commitment, you need to consider and plan for the impact that will have on your staff. There may be responsibilities that need to be delegated while you are out, or you may need to be clear on who can make decisions in your absence.

Marcus, vice president of a small technology company, had little choice but to quickly seek assistance. A motorcycle enthusiast who took regular weekend rides through rugged mountain roads, Marcus took a bad spill and wound up in the hospital for two weeks. First, he needed help getting well. He and his surgeon found a physical therapist who could work with Marcus to regain his mobility. Then, Marcus needed help taking care of all his usual tasks. He and his wife worked through temporary help for home and community commitments. That left work.

He arranged a call with his team, to talk through who had the time, skills, and willingness to pick up some of his work, and discuss what tasks he could do from home. They realized that it wasn't the day-to-day work that would be an issue—among the group they could manage it—but rather finding someone who could be a "face" to the client. No one on the team felt comfortable assuming that role. Together, they brainstormed a short list of people who might help, and what support the team would need to offer the "stand-in."

Once he came back to work, Marcus continued to rely on his team and stand-in. Initially, he only worked three days a week, needing the other two for physical therapy. Ultimately, though, he was back at full speed, and had the added benefit of a more skilled and confident team.

WHAT WILL HELP YOU GET THERE?

Talents are our natural abilities, aptitudes, behaviors, or ways of thinking that we can productively apply to our life's experiences. Unfortunately, many of us have focused more on improving our weaknesses than on identifying and using our talents. But it's the unique talents and gifts that you innately possess that will get you where you want to go. (Buckingham and Clifton, 2001)

How do you discover your talents? Chances are they are in use every day in some way, and with a little thought, you can easily identify them. For example:

- *They are found in those tasks that you take for granted.* Those things you do easily, often unaware of the talents that you're using. For example, if you can easily envision how the pieces of a whole will connect—a puzzle, an unassembled toy, or a flow chart—then that is one of your talents. It also can come in handy in organizing the pages of a presentation or the chapters of a book. You find these tasks easy and do them without thinking much about what talents they require.
- *They are used in the tasks you enjoy.* You anticipate and look forward to activities that use your talents. If you finish a project and find yourself thinking "When can I do this again?" or "I wish I could do more of that," you were using some of your talents and gifts. If, on the other hand, you finish a project or task thinking "I'm glad that's over," and would prefer to hand it off

to someone else in the future, it probably required some talents that you might not have, or don't enjoy using.

- *Others seek you out for those talents.* Others may recognize and tap in to your talents even though you are unaware of them, especially if it's a talent they don't possess. They notice how easily or quickly you are able to accomplish something and seek you out again.

Consider how your talents and abilities will combine to help you achieve the results you envision, not just through work but through all your life domains.

BE REFLECTIVE AND MAKE CONNECTIONS

Consider the implications of your choices. Think about what each of your choices really means both for you and for others.

How do choices in one life domain affect another? Perhaps you've decided that you really do want to complete the education that was interrupted. Ask yourself what that might mean financially, or for the relationships that you want to develop, or for your leisure activities, or for your current work situation. Remember, no single choice is an independent piece; all of these choices combine to form your life.

Consider a choice facing Jonathan. He was newly wed, had a demanding job, and was teaching art on the side. He and his wife worked hard and were saving to buy a house. Though involved in a few community groups, he wasn't as active as he'd like to be. One night he got a call from someone he knew at a local nonprofit organization. The caller asked Jonathan if he would consider working with the program directors, that they needed some new ideas and new energy. It would be a paid position (always a plus). His initial reaction was to say yes, but he decided to talk it through with his wife. They discussed what the time commitment would be, how else he might help the organization, and what adding yet another outside activity would mean for their relationship. After reflecting on it,

Jonathan decided that if he said yes, he would be taking on too much, and would not meet his existing commitments in the way he wanted. He phoned back and declined the offer.

How will your choices affect your own mental, physical, emotional, or spiritual well-being? You can't do it all, and the purpose of a personal vision is not to see how much *more* you can do, but instead, to help you to make choices about what you will do and what you will not do. Get others' input. They interact with you on a daily basis and their perspective of how well you're currently doing and how these choices will affect you may be different from your own.

In a similar vein, you do not lead an independent life. As you explore and clarify your values and vision, you should engage those who are close to you—both for their advice and perspective as well as to compare how their aims mesh with yours. Find the synergies and common aspirations, and find ways to support one another.

Robin was a former high school French teacher. She resigned after 20 years, even though she had secured tenure and would have received a modest pension at age 65. The decision was not easy, especially for her family, because she had carried health insurance for all three of them. The departmental in-fighting, the constant budget crisis, the increasing disinterest of students, and the complaining parents—they left Robin frequently tired, and even depressed. It had become clear to both her daughter and her husband that Robin had lost the passion for teaching, so they encouraged her to pursue other options.

Robin wanted to open a framing shop, turning what had been a hobby into a small business. The planning that went into this family change had been extensive; Robin often joked that no military commander could have thought more strategically for so long. Her daughter would be covered by college insurance, her husband by his company insurance, and she would buy her own through her earnings. With the lease paid for one year in advance, she could work without fear for many months, getting the word out in the town that her products were great. Each time she finished a frame, cut the glass, and looked at the final product, Robin felt enormous satisfaction.

HELP OTHERS WITH THE PROCESS

Just as staying focused and getting results is not about fitting more into your personal agenda, it is also not accomplished for others simply by commanding that it happen. Jack Welch, former CEO of General Electric, has been quoted as saying, "We have to undo a 100-year-old concept and convince our managers that their role is not to control people and stay 'on top' of things, but rather to guide, energize, and excite." This is not to imply that you don't still need to get work done and generate results, because you do. But you will generate the *best* solutions and the *best* results when people are truly engaged with what they do. "Great," you may be thinking, "I agree, but how do I do that?"

In addition to finding your own center of equilibrium, do you understand where others want to be at the current chapter in their lives? Do you know what they most value? Do you understand their unique combination of talents, skills, and gifts? Do you engage in honest conversations with those you lead to help them think about their goals and aspirations, and what is most important to them? Have you helped give them a framework for thinking about what they value and why? Your ability to guide, energize, and excite depends on the degree to which you are able to explore their vision, values, and talents, and the degree to which they are willing to share.

Remember Miranda and your own stories of chaos that came to mind as you read her story? The people who you manage may be experiencing the same difficulties in gaining self-insight. Integrating their various life domains, figuring out what is most important to them at this chapter in their lives, understanding what they value, and discovering and bringing to bear their talents and gifts isn't simple. These techniques will help both you as an individual and you as a manager who is responsible for guiding, energizing, exciting, and focusing others.

CHECKLIST

❏ What are some key things you envision accomplishing within the current chapter of your life?

❏ Identify the two or three equilibrium points that will be your foundation for this chapter.
  • Who is affected by your choices?
  • Whose support or help do you need?

❏ How will you manage your priorities, time, and energy around these items?
  • What changes will you make?
  • What resources do you need?

❏ How can you help others gain equilibrium through assessing their vision, values, or talents?

CHAPTER THREE

GUIDING, ENERGIZING, AND EXCITING

IN THIS CHAPTER

Finding Leverage ■ Goal Setting ■ Calibration
Points ■ Measures of Success

In the book *First Things First,* the authors describe the contrast between two powerful tools that can direct us—the clock and the compass. A clock represents how we manage our time—appointments, schedules, etc.—and a compass represents how we manage our life domains—what we feel is important and how we live our lives. (Covey, Merrill, and Merrill, 1994)

If we placed our life domains around a type of "life compass," those domains that are most important at this chapter in time become our guiding points as we consider our vision of where we want to go, the core values and beliefs that define what is important to us, and the unique talents and gifts that will enable us to get there. We can then reinforce our life choices with goals, calibration points, measures, behaviors, symbols, and routines. Unlike a real compass, where the guiding needle sits firmly on N as we move around, our life compass has multiple points of guidance as we transition and focus on the various domains.

FIGURE 3.1 The Life Compass

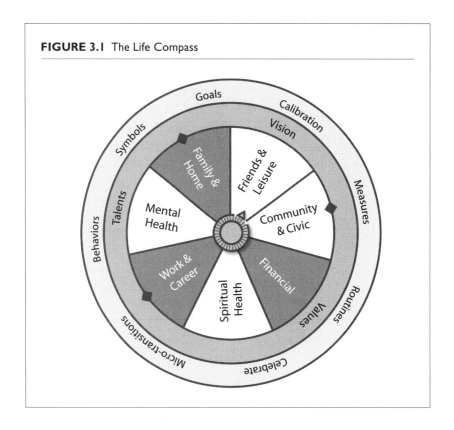

FINDING LEVERAGE

What have you discovered about yourself through constructing your vision, testing your values, and engaging others for their input? One thing you've likely discovered is that there are more items on your "want to do" list than will fit into your life, and that you will have to make choices.

The same applies when you step back and assess all of the things that you and your team would like to accomplish. Even after you identify the truly important or urgent items, there simply may be more to do than one person or one team can accomplish at one time, especially when there are any number of factors working to divert their focus.

As we said, the goal is certainly not to fit it *all* in, or even to fit *more* in. How do you decide what stays? Concentrate on where you can gain the most leverage now. "Leverage" has become somewhat of an overused term in management today. *It's really about picking the few things that will make the most difference and have the most impact today.* This is a critical concept to remember. Concentrate on "a few things," because you can't do it all. The items that will *make the most difference* and *have the most impact* will be those things that cross organizational boundaries and even go beyond the organization itself. You must engage with others both to understand the effect of the results you envision and to incorporate their experiences and expertise. Finally, focus on the interval you are in, the impact *today*. Have a vision of the future, but manage today.

As a manager you need to consider where you and your team can get the most leverage; that is, where you get the most benefit for the effort, time, and resources you use. Leverage can come from many sources. It can come from doing two things at once. It can come from planning before acting, so you get pretty close to the desired outcome the first time. It can come from taking smaller steps that make the bigger steps easier. Imagine that you are literally the manager in the center, the person in control of multiple levers that can generate results, but you can only select a few levers, maybe two or three. Ask yourself, "What would I have if I could accomplish these two or three things? Which would make the most difference for the organization, for my team, and for me?" As you consider these two questions:

- *Think sequence.* Focus on the present chapter that you or others are in, with an eye toward the future. It's not always a question of yes or no when considering whether to take on tasks, but when. Something that may not be a key leverage point today can take on more significance later.
- *Think synergy.* Across the various life domains, where can you or others combine efforts? Is there a sequence that builds on naturally occurring events?
- *Think sustainable.* Some tasks will be building a foundation, and their benefits won't be immediately visible to others. These tasks are still important.

- *Think alignment.* What are you or your group doing today that supports a future vision?

Once you have those two or three "levers" identified, you can begin to think about the choices you will have to make when presented with opportunities. How will your choices regarding priorities, time, energy, or resources support your efforts? Gaining leverage is also about connecting with and engaging other people. If they are affected by your choices or if you will need their support, then they need to agree with your choices as well. Finally, remember that the world is dynamic and so are all the domains of our lives; consider your plans as a work in progress and be prepared to be flexible.

Identifying your equilibrium bearings and selecting key levers and priorities for your team will give direction, but ultimately, this still doesn't get the work done. Look back to the two or three important items that you personally identified in Chapter 2. You probably know from experience that simply saying something is important isn't enough to produce results. You also need some practical methods to help you and others stay focused and engaged on the results you are trying to create. Defining clear goals, regular calibration points, and measures of success will help you stay the course you've charted.

GOAL SETTING

Goals are one way to operationalize priorities into more manageable pieces that people can make progress on. If equilibrium points, vision, and priorities provide the larger context, then goals help guide the day-to-day work and decision making. For example, let's say that one of your priorities is to retire at age 55. If that phase of your life is still quite a few years away, it's difficult to stay focused. Creating goals that are 1 year out, 5 years out, and 10 years out gives you manageable pieces to work on and clarifies what you need to do *now*. These goals are also more likely to fit with your current life domains. One of your 1-year goals might be to increase your savings account by a certain percentage or to finish the last few courses of your degree. The end vision is still in sight (enough savings for retirement or graduating), but the more immediate goals drive your action and help you stay focused.

Most organizations have some type of formal goal-setting process, and people have informal goals as well. You've likely worked through some type of goal-setting activity either in assessing your own goals or in guiding someone else through the process. Goal setting is a process for deciding what you are trying to achieve as a team and as an individual. Ideally, an organization and its employees have compatible goals, that is, ones that both support the vision and strategic plan of the organization (after all, you want your company to succeed) and also support individual values, interests, and personal development (you want to achieve individual success as well).

If "guiding, energizing, and exciting," is in fact our mantra, how should we approach goal setting?

Begin with Clear and Specific Outcomes

Whether you subscribe to a goal-setting model such as SMART (Specific, Measurable, Actionable, Realistic, Timely) or another set of guidelines, the point is to be as clear as possible. What *exactly* do you want to accomplish? How will you know if you've accomplished what you wanted; what is the measure? Is the goal actionable—that is, do you understand both what the end result is and what you need to do? Is it realistic—something you are both *willing* and *able* to work toward and truly *believe* can be accomplished? Is there a time frame and a target endpoint to work toward? If you don't set a time frame, your commitment to the goal is more likely to be weakened because there is no sense of urgency. The simple exercise of *writing down* your goals (rather than just thinking or talking about them) will help you to give them more definition.

Remember Miranda from Chapter 1? Her life was an unmediated blur—research, family, schedules, obligations, and clients all swirled around her on a daily basis. Even with an online calendar and an assistant, Miranda lived erratically, in a constant, reactive state of just-in-time response. A multitude of tasks clamored for her attention, but she had no real vision helping to guide her decisions and actions. In the midst of a meeting, she'd recall that she hadn't arranged a babysitter for the school board meeting, and begin making notes to do so (sometimes not really listening to what others were saying). At the school board meeting, she'd be thinking about the next day's client or the unfinished laundry at home. Each weekend, she would promise herself that she would plan the upcoming week's activities, prioritize them, and have the discipline to stick to her plan. Yet nothing seemed to change, except her level of ever-diminishing energy and ever-increasing list of tasks left undone. Creating some specific goals to start the week, even small ones, could begin to help her gain some sense of control and stay focused on the results she wants to achieve.

"We're a great team, Sash—you with your small and large motor skills, me with my spatial awareness and hand-eye coördination."

Focus on Talents, Skills, and Knowledge, and Not on Weaknesses

People are different, each bringing a unique combination of talents and gifts to use. Skills are about knowing how to do something, which can be taught. Knowledge is about the information, understanding, or connections that you have "discovered" through your own experiences and study. We can teach skills, we can create opportunities for people to extend their knowledge, and we can guide them in developing challenging goals that will help them grow in both areas. However, talents and gifts are more innate. Sometimes they're obvious and recognized by the rest of the team. Other times, they're waiting to be discovered.

Perhaps you can help in this process. All three can be applied to the work at hand. What work will most energize and excite your people? This is really an exercise in *discovery,* understanding some of what each team member brings to the table that can benefit both you as the manager and the other team members. For example, answer the following questions:

- What do they know how to do?
- What prior experiences are useful to the work at hand?
- What are they really good at?
- What most engages their imagination and creativity?
- What do they want to do more of or learn more about?
- What type of lifestyle are they trying to create at this phase of their life?
- When are they at their best on the job?

Is one person naturally good at organizing? Take, for example, Caleb, a former Air Force helicopter pilot who is now working as an associate at a small hedge fund company. One of the group's senior partners recognized within two months of hiring Caleb that he was innately gifted in time management, so she assigned him to schedule and facilitate the group's biweekly, four-hour meetings. No one showed up late after that, no time was wasted, and no nerves were frayed. Caleb's experience, maturity, and skills were used perfectly, and he got great satisfaction from keeping the meetings on schedule and on topic—a role that no one else was eager to assume.

Remember, you need to invest time in building relationships and connecting with others. Finding and maintaining your own bearings and focus depend on these connections. You need to know what you can do for others and what they are best able to help you with. It's about reciprocity, not just about what's in it for you. If you don't spend time engaging them, you will not succeed. Consider what we know about Miranda's relationships and support system. We know that she has a husband and children, and that she has a personal assistant at work. With the number of tasks and responsibilities that she's attempting to juggle, she needs to invest some time in thinking about those around her—what she does, what they do, and if they should make adjustments. By using her support systems well, she can help herself and others.

Be Flexible and Creative in Finding the Right Fit

Finding the right alignment and blend of the outcomes you are trying to achieve, the capabilities and competencies you need, and what each person possesses in terms of knowledge, strengths, talents, and personal goals can be a bit like experimenting with a new recipe. For example, if your team needs to develop a new competency, experiment with finding who has some natural talents in that area. Challenge them with stretch goals; you may find out that one person wasn't quite the right fit but also discover a hidden talent in another. Like a recipe, you try a little more of this and a little less of that until you find the combination that works. Remember, while it may work for now, it may need adjusting over time.

Allow People to Find Their Own Way

Define the right outcomes, assign accountability, and check progress on goals—but let individuals use their own methods for getting there. Three different people, given the same goal, may take three different paths to the end result, and none may be the path you would have taken. Recognize that their different aspirations, skills, knowledge, and talents will help define the route that they take.

Thomas Gladwin, an anthropologist, compared how a native Trukese and a European sailor each navigated small boats between tiny Pacific islands (Paredes and Hepburn, 1976). The Trukese relied on his mental map of the islands and intuitive feel for the sea. He continually observed the relative positions of landmarks, sun, wind direction, and ocean conditions. He navigated comparing where he started, where he was going, and where he was now, improvising the best path as he went. In contrast, the European relies on a plotted course, planned using charts, maps, compass, and sextant. He methodically moved through the plan step by step, measuring and comparing current position against the plan. Both sailors got where they're going, but had a different process to get there. Combining these seemingly paradoxical skills is imperative. Plan your chapters, and improvise your journey.

CALIBRATION POINTS

If letting people "find their own path" to the desired outcome gives you some pause, don't worry. Similar to the notion of intervals or chapters in your life, build in smaller intervals to reflect on where you or your group is and where you're going. Calibration points along the way can be used to gauge progress, assess the current path you're taking, realign with your vision for this interval, and assess how people are doing. Some of the priorities that you've identified may not actually come to fruition for quite some time; using just a long-term vision of the future to stay focused is difficult and risky given that the end results can feel very far away.

Your goals should not only break a larger task into manageable pieces but they also should provide some natural calibration points. As we'll discuss later, you should routinely touch base to get a reading on how well a project is progressing or how well an individual is performing in his or her role. Concentrate on a vision for the chapter that you're in and build in regular calibration points to stay focused and realign if needed.

Whether you call them temperature checks, milestones, or calibration points, the idea is to create a pause in the action and assess where you are and where you're going—in terms of work and people. Use this time to have conversations with people, not just to assess data. The purpose is not to have people feel as if you are "checking up" on them to verify that they are working hard, nor is it to create policy or procedures to "control" anything outside the norm. The purpose of calibration points is to reassess where you want to be (your vision) and where you are today (your current situation). Then you can account for and adjust to inevitable changes, such as changes in strategy, priorities, milestones, and dates, and to changes in the people themselves.

Depending on the scope of the work and the level of challenge it presents for the individuals, there may be small calibration points (once a week or month perhaps), midsize calibration points (every couple of months), and a larger, more extensive calibration that occurs once per year. Here are some questions you might ask when stopping to calibrate.

- *How is the work progressing?* Consider the rate and quality of the progress. Assess if there have been unexpected delays or whether the right people are involved. For example, did the phone conference get delayed because of technical difficulties? Are vendor deliveries arriving reliably? Are the time lines still reasonable?
- *Do we have what we need to do the work?* Evaluate your resources and budgeting, as they were originally set up and now that you are in the midst of it. Do you have what you need to succeed? For example, has everyone received the proposal draft as prom-

ised? Did the new equipment arrive and is it working well? Are individuals clear about their deliverables and meeting their deadlines?

- *Are there signs of struggle?* Difficulties may arise among project team members or individuals may struggle with their assignments. Does silence from a team member indicate that all is on track, or does it signify reluctance to admit difficulty? Does silence mean nothing? Are people staying at work later than normal? Have there been tense moments in team meetings? If so, what can you do to help them regain their forward momentum? Perhaps a personal phone call or lunch away from the office (rather than an impersonal e-mail) will provide an opportunity to discuss and better understand what people are struggling with.

- *Have our priorities or goals changed?* Sometimes, unexpected things happen. Priorities are shifted. Resources get reassigned. Target dates or parameters are moved. For example, just as people are making some progress on a project, a shift in priorities, an unexpected budget item, or changing client needs may mean you have to stop and realign. People may decide to make shifts in their other life domains that will affect how they want to approach work, or what work they want to do. People's lives change constantly—they move, they get married, they have children, they have aging parents in bad health, they have spouses who are out of work. The schedules and routines that worked well for them in the past may have to adjust for new circumstances. Be creative and flexible in adapting to these changes.

- *Does the team need help beyond its boundaries?* How well is the team managing relationships beyond the core team? As the team's leader, is there anything you need to do to coordinate, integrate, communicate, or negotiate with external stakeholders? Perhaps only one person responds to a request that was sent out to the external stakeholders. Does that mean he is the designated spokesperson, or is he just assuming that role? Maybe he is just the most vocal. Perhaps an external event that you are unaware of is keeping people from responding, such as

a companywide event or a major client problem. Can you follow up with others personally to see why they haven't responded? (See our book *Influencing and Collaborating for
Results* for additional tips on building a network of relationships and collaborating across boundaries.)

- *How are you doing?* You need to occasionally stop and calibrate
  how you are doing as an individual as well as a leader. Consider
  your personal visions and priorities. Consider the goals and
  priorities that you have as a leader. How are you progressing?
  Are you still aligned with what is most important? What adjustments do you need to make? Is your support system working?
  Often, we try to store all that we need to do in our memory
  banks, tapping our heads and saying, "I've got it right here."
  Because you're thinking about that list all the time, you may
  think that you have done more than you actually have. Give
  yourself deadlines, too, and don't go too easy on yourself. Perform a "brain dump" on paper—the act of writing out the competing thoughts, lists, and deadlines may help you recognize
  what's still missing or what additional steps need to be taken.

MEASURES OF SUCCESS

*"Success comes from doing what you enjoy.
If you don't enjoy it, how can it be called success?"*
(Maister, 2000)

When you or your team members reach a goal, take the time to
enjoy the satisfaction of having accomplished the goal. Think about
the implications and note the progress you've made, especially how
much closer you now are to other goals. If the goal was a significant
one, reward yourself.

Measure and Reward the Important Things

In the now-famous article *On the Folly of Rewarding A, While Hoping for B,* there are multiple examples across society and business—politics, medicine, universities, etc.—where the rewards we put in place don't reward the behaviors that are actually most important. In one company example, performance ratings affected the annual merit raise by only 1 percent: excellent was worth 5 percent, above average 4 percent, and negligent and irresponsible was 3 percent. On the other hand, excessive absences in a six-month period could result in losing the full percentage. The end result is that they were hoping for performance, but rewarding attendance. (Kerr, 1975) What are the effects of rewarding the wrong action? The energy and excitement that you've worked to build can be quickly disipated.

You work within a larger performance management culture, and certain elements are beyond your control, but you do control the culture and environment of your own team. What are you doing to create an environment that does measure and reward the behavior that you and your team have agreed are most important?

Be Aware That Success Has Multiple Views

Just as individuals have different perspectives on their life domains, different priorities for this moment of their life, and different goals, their views of success will vary as well.

- *Success has a personal view.* How do individuals gauge the way that a project went or the personal progress that they made? As individuals, we all have different starting points. A beginner's view of success will be very different than that of a seasoned veteran.
- *Success has a collective view,* based on how others view the end result. How does the team view the results? Was it critical to deliver on time and did you make the deadline? Is the client happy with the design? Are customers buying the new product?

- *Success has a leadership view.* Of course you want successful results for the team and the organization. But some of those results will be qualitative and by-products of the project itself: how well the team has worked together, and how much individuals have improved a skill or developed knowledge.
- *Can you achieve the desired results and still not feel successful?* Many things can affect your view of success:
  - The tradeoffs (and agreement to make them) around deliverables and deadlines
  - The amount of time invested, especially time away from other priorities. Was it worth it?
  - Amount of input and freedom people have to work independently
  - Disagreements or tensions that have emerged among team members or with other stakeholders

Celebrate Multiple Levels of Success

Success will come in parts and pieces, just like goals. Reaching the ultimate goal or vision is not the only measure of success. Just as there are differing goals and priorities for individuals, teams, and the organization, there are multiple views of success as well. Recognize the outstanding efforts of individuals, the group accomplishments of the team, and the organizational results that are an outgrowth of their efforts.

Marcus, the VP of the small technology company from Chapter 2, brings bagels and cream cheese to the office on Friday mornings as a tradition denoting the end of the workweek. As employees arrive, they stand around munching on bagels and talking about their weekend plans, the weather, or some sports events. Marcus makes a point of noting all of the accomplishments of the past week as well, letting them know that he is aware of and noting these accomplishments. Scattering off to their desks 15–20 minutes later than usual hurts little, and they attack their day's activities with a bit more energy and focus.

Motivating the performance of others requires understanding their beliefs, their needs, and what they value—that is, what will energize and excite them. They aren't motivated just because you tell them to be. People won't be engaged for the same reasons, measure success in the same way, or be motivated by the same rewards.

There are both intrinsic and extrinsic motivating factors at work. Intrinsic motivation defines *what people will do without external inducement*—when you do something because it is challenging, interesting, personally rewarding, or because you believe in it. Extrinsic motivators are external factors that have an effect on your behavior—often the tangible reward of something that you desire.

You may immediately think "money" when we mention extrinsic motivators, but that isn't the full story. Remember all of the life domains and the elements that are most valued by people. In the book *1001 Ways to Reward Employees,* the authors' interviews with over 600 employees and managers revealed that some of the best motivators cost little or nothing (Blanchard, Nelson, and Schudlich, 1994):

- Sincere and timely praise

- Autonomy/flexibility

- Learning and growth opportunities

- Recognition among peers

Don't Ignore Your Personal Success and Rewards

Too often it seems that unless you define success for yourself, it gets defined for you. Then you begin gauging your own success based on the expectations and calculations of others. How would *you* complete the following sentences?

- "I consider myself successful when . . ."
- "The most important reward for me is . . ."

Has this always been your view? Who or what have been important influences in shaping your view of success? Do you measure success regularly—daily, weekly, yearly?

Marcus holds three clear visions of a successful week. As a company manager, has he spoken, personally, with all seven direct reports? He'll start with a generic question about a project, then sit down and listen for 10–15 minutes to the employee's thoughts, concerns, and questions. He knows that by serving as a sounding board, and listening actively and nonjudgmentally, the person speaking actually articulates ideas that may have just been floating around as a sense of unease.

His second measure is whether he has touched base with his clients, even if they are not expecting a call or an e-mail. He does this so that they always know that they are on his radar. Finally, he evaluates his family's mood by calling home often, to just chat with the kids and listen to summaries of their day and hear their plans. Even if he has to work late on a particular night, they know and he knows that they are an integrated unit of trust and care.

CHECKLIST

- ❏ Review the goals that exist today for you, the individuals who report to you, and the collective team.
  - Talk about the goals.
  - Write them down.
  - Make them SMART.
- ❏ Make sure that you have created frequent calibration points.
- ❏ Assess whether you are measuring and rewarding the most important things behaviors and outcomes.
- ❏ Regularly take time to celebrate milestones and successes.

CHAPTER FOUR

THE VALUE OF ROUTINES

IN THIS CHAPTER

Life Routines ▪ Building Work Routines ▪ Show Them How It's
Done ▪ Don't Forget the Fun Stuff ▪ Renewal and Flexibility

> *Without habit a man might be occupied all day in dressing and*
> *undressing himself; the attitude of his body would absorb all his*
> *attention and energy; the washing of his hands or the fastening*
> *of a button would be as difficult to him on each occasion as to*
> *the child on its first trial; and he would furthermore, be*
> *completely exhausted by his exertions.*
> William James

LIFE ROUTINES

Sit back and think about the word *routine* for a moment. What
kinds of routines are part of your life? If you exercise regularly, you
probably follow a workout routine. If you are a parent, you may follow a routine with your kids each evening to help keep them on
track—dinner, bath, story, bed. Each of us probably has some type of
morning routine, such as waking up around the same time and getting ready for the day in a predictable order: shower, dress, paper,
coffee, and out the door. How many of us routinely drive the same
route to work each day, to the point that we feel as if we are on auto-
matic pilot—not really needing to think about where we need to turn,
and sometimes not remembering the drive?

Routines Help Get the Easier Stuff Out of the Way

Without planning it or even realizing it, most of us settle into routines with the tasks that we do regularly. We don't approach routine activities by doing *exactly* the same thing in the same way each time, but we do develop some general patterns that help us along. After all, if we began each day by stopping to think and make choices about what to do next and how to do it—getting dressed, cooking breakfast, or preparing lunches—we'd never make it to work on time. Routines make more room for the challenging stuff—those tasks that are more interesting, more engaging, more unusual, more important, or more difficult—yet let us be sure to get our day-to-day activities done.

Routines Reinforce Our Priorities

We create some routines to protect the things we've decided *are* important to us at this chapter in our life, such as volunteer activities, religious rituals, time with family, and, yes, time at work. For example, when one of the authors of this book was a child, she had breakfast out most Saturday mornings with her father. That routine gave them time with one another, and it was her dad's way of letting her know that she was special. We create these routines to ensure that those things are not forgotten or pushed aside by other demands. Otherwise, we can find big gaps between what we *say* matters most and what we actually do. Without some routines to help keep us aligned, it's easy to look back at the end of the month and find that we *didn't* spend our time or money or effort or attention on what we said mattered most. Maintaining routines around our priorities sends us a reinforcing message and declares to others what indeed is still important.

Routines Help You Work toward Your Goals

Athletes maintain training routines not because they always enjoy them, but because they help achieve a primary goal: being the most prepared physically and mentally to compete. Feeling better physically or losing those extra pounds helps motivate people to maintain their exercise routines. The desire to deliver a flawless performance—acting, singing, dancing—motivates a performer to adhere to a practice or rehearsal routine. Whatever the goal we have, when we see some improvement or progress toward our goal, it reinforces the benefits of routines.

Although they vary in purpose and scope, at some level all routines are about planning, structure, and stability. To actually be effective, they also require some degree of discipline and follow-through. An athlete who charts a detailed exercise routine that begins with a four-mile run still has to actually get out of bed, get dressed, go through warm-ups, and complete the run. Similarly, you can plan any number of routines—weekly team meetings, blocks of time for responding to e-mail or making personal calls to clients—but you have to have the discipline to follow through and make them happen.

BUILDING WORK ROUTINES

For the same reasons we find them useful in our personal lives, routines also can have significant value in our work lives. At the end of your day, do you feel as if there was no structure, no stability, but more a series of events and crises and chaos that you simply reacted to and tried to stay ahead of? If so, chances are that members of your team may be feeling the same way. Used effectively, routines can help you and those who you lead get the easier tasks out of the way, align and reinforce your priorities, and stay focused on your goals and objectives. Rather than thinking about using routines as a way to fit *more* into the day, consider them as a way to ensure that what you *said* was most important isn't lost in the chaos. *Routines help direct attention and effort*. Thus, the critical choice for leaders isn't whether to have routines but it's which routines to have. (Kouzes and Posner, 2002)

Routines created to streamline the easy stuff should help to get it done and also help to save time, so that you and your people can focus on more challenging, engaging, and energizing tasks. Consider the various items pending for your group today that you wouldn't describe as difficult or critical but that still need to be done on a regular basis. Often times, other groups or areas within the company are dependent on the output of your tasks in order to effectively do their jobs. The accounting department needs the recent travel expense reports; the business development office needs all new account projections; HR needs the quarterly staff evaluations; clients need to be billed but the team project manager who is out of town hasn't generated the invoices; and the weekly status reports for your boss are late. There's nothing here that can't wait "one more day," but with all of the "critical" items that fill the day, your team seems to have a difficult time *ever* getting around to these items. You can probably predict what happens next—you get a phone call about the items that are late and they get escalated to "urgent" status. They aren't really important to you; they're just late. You and your team may end up spending significant time on these items when your attention really does need to be focused on something more important.

However, routines can help complete the easy or day-to-day work, so that you can spend time on and pay attention to the more complex or exciting tasks. Think about why you have trouble getting a particular task completed, even when it's easy, and whether creating a different routine or changing the approach might solve the problem. For example, ask yourself these questions as a way to figure out how routines could move work forward.

- *Which items can be scheduled in advance?* You just may need a reminder for certain action items. If you schedule predictable events in advance rather than as they occur, they can be dealt with quickly and efficiently. For example, if new account projections are due every three months, schedule a recurring "reminder" lunch meeting for those involved. This way, those responsible for the projections report can be pleasantly told again.

- *Where can you bundle and leverage effort?* Let's say you schedule those "reminder" lunch meetings every three months. Can you also prompt team members to bring along their current project status reports as well? Putting several things together as one "chore" eliminates multiple preparations, multiple meetings, and multiple delays.

- *Are there predictable bottlenecks?* If it seems like there must be an easier way, there probably is. For example, if team members seem to always be late to an early morning meeting after long, three-day week-ends, think about creating a different routine, such as arranging the meeting time in late afternoon instead of morning. That can relieve the early morning time pressures as well as break up the low-energy late afternoons.

- *Are the right people on the tasks?* If a particular task is not one you are good at or enjoy, more discipline and more routines won't necessarily help the situation. Consider how people's talents, skills, and gifts best align with the work that needs to be done. Shift tasks to those who have talent at that task, such as creating client proposals or managing project budgets, or to those who are interested in and aspire to develop in that area.

Your group shares a common view of the top priorities, but when you take stock at the end of the week, month, or year, other lower-priority items seem to have consumed all of your time and energy. This can be especially hard when the priority deliverables are well in the future and it feels as if there's still plenty of time to worry about that later. Remember, important is *not* the same as urgent. For many of us, reacting to urgent things has become a way of life, and at the end of the day we judge our value by how many crises we managed to avert rather than on our progress toward long-term goals and objectives. And very few of us measure how engaging, energizing, or "fun" our day was.

FIGURE 4.1 Time Management Matrix

	Urgent	Not Urgent
Important	**Work:** key client requests and project deadlines **Physical Health:** **Spiritual Health:** **Home/Family:** **Friends/Leisure:** **Financial:** **Civic/Community:**	**Work:** strategic planning, team goals, coaching, building capability **Physical Health:** **Spiritual Health:** **Home/Family:** **Friends/Leisure:** **Financial:** **Civic/Community:**
Not Important	**Work:** weekly reports and meetings **Physical Health:** **Spiritual Health:** **Home/Family:** **Friends/Leisure:** **Financial:** **Civic/Community:**	**Work:** junk mail, phone calls, cleaning your desk **Physical Health:** **Spiritual Health:** **Home/Family:** **Friends/Leisure:** **Financial:** **Civic/Community:**

The Time Management Matrix shown in Figure 4.1 proposes that there are two factors that we can use to categorize our activities: urgency and importance. (Covey, 1989) Typically when we see an example of this type of matrix, the quadrants are filled with work items; however, that approach still assumes that we can easily separate our life domains. *Consider where elements of all of your life domains fit into the matrix at this interval of your life.*

How can you make sure that enough of your energy is spent on important, not urgent things? What types of routines help you reinforce your priorities and make progress toward your goals and objectives? Consider the following:

- *Set aside and protect blocks of time.* Much like you might reserve one night a week for family time, carve out an hour or more within the workday and focus first on what's important. This gives you enough time to focus your full attention rather than sporadically catching a minute here or there. You might use this block to have one-on-one coaching conversations with staff, plan and schedule necessary training, or follow up with your boss on a new strategic direction of your division. Don't allow these blocks to be removed. For example, our friend Marcus from Chapter 2, will not let a week pass without his "sit and listen" time with employees. For Marcus, it provides a time when he doesn't have to talk, direct, decide, or evaluate. He can sit and absorb. For the workers, who prepare detailed training manuals or listen to clients' needs all day, these times allow them to express themselves, one-on-one, to a willing listener. They can talk about frustrations, obstacles, or accomplishments, or tell humorous anecdotes and stories. It breaks up the day for all concerned.

- *Establish short-term deliverables, action items, or deadlines.* Deadlines, even if self-imposed, have a way of giving more substance to a project and keeping attention focused on it. Think back to your academic days. Large assignments, such as term papers or projects, had a way of slipping to the back of the list until the deadline loomed. Milestones help keep people engaged and offer an opportunity to provide feedback. Working for long periods without short-term deliverables can tend to disengage others from the process. Reporting weekly on progress may also help to include and keep others engaged; updates and progress reports provide nice breaking points for input and feedback.

- *Use different visual and technical reinforcements.* These techniques can help keep you from spilling over into times set aside for other items. One office manager we know sets her timer for 30 minutes when answering e-mail, a task that can easily consume hours if she doesn't structure that time. Additionally, each Monday, the office manager writes notes in bright red ink on a big whiteboard set in her office. She lists the activities she must accomplish that week that her online calendar does not include. The whiteboard reminds her to update those files on her chair, read the new issue of a professional journal, and touch base with existing clients.

• *Renew, reconnect, and rejuvenate.* Let's be realistic. You know that you can plan and create priorities and reserve time, but things happen. There are periods where one domain takes over your life and everything else takes a backseat: A family member has a serious illness or injury, so your focus on work priorities wanes. We have to turn tasks over to others or change deadlines. For many of us, it's more frequently the case that there are periods where our work is the most demanding domain and consumes most of our time and attention. If you spend weeks (or months) putting extreme amounts of focus and energy on something (a client presentation, a new product launch, an organizational restructuring), build in time to recover, restore, and renew when it ends. Realistically, you may not be able to take a two-week vacation, but you can schedule a smaller interval break. Take the afternoon off or take a long weekend for reflection, renewal, and refocusing.

Can routines go too far? Yes. In 1973, the third crew of the Skylab Space Station staged a strike in space. They turned off their radio and stopped communicating with Houston Mission Control at the end of their sixth week in orbit. There were varying opinions as to why this group of highly-trained and disciplined astronauts rebelled— the length of their stay, the cramped work area, the effects of a low gravity environment—but a major reason was the amount of structured routines that those on the ground tried to impose on them.

Mission Control was proud of how much they could achieve by laying out the whole day for the astronauts. Pages and pages were sent to them every day—at least 42 separate instructions—telling the astronauts when to eat, when to exercise, and precisely when to conduct experiments. NASA was constantly communicating through the radio and Houston taped everything.

For various reasons, this third crew got off to a slower start than the other two missions and frequently found they were falling behind "schedule." Everyone had agreed not to schedule as hectic a pace as that followed by the second Skylab crew; however, from the beginning, ground control started picking up the pace and was soon expecting the crew to be doing the same amount of work as the previous crew. The astronauts had only ten minutes to move from one experiment to the next, a short time given they never had done the exercise previously. This pressure was exacerbated by the fact that the previous crews had not been good housekeepers. Some *forty thousand* items were stowed in over a hundred cabinets in the space station, however, items were not in the right place, cabinets were not labeled well, and the crew spent valuable time just trying to find what they needed.

Some of the ground crew recommended easing up. Yet in an effort to catch up, ground control began scheduling experiments during time that was supposed to be reserved for the astronauts—meal times together, exercise time, and the 8 to 10 PM period that was supposed to be their personal time to use however they wanted. All of these time blocks were supposedly recognized as valuable and important, but still became packed with other "must do" activities. Ground control thought they were helping the astronauts catch up and be as efficient as possible. They set a schedule to get the most out of the time the crew had. Unfortunately, they missed the downside: Instead of helping, the tight schedule caused needless stress. A routine should not stifle, and a schedule shouldn't become a straightjacket.

And so, for one day, the crew rebelled. They turned off the radio, stopped working, and spent the entire day doing whatever they felt like doing. (McCaskey and Balbaky, 1981)

SHOW THEM HOW IT'S DONE

Work routines aren't just about keeping *others* engaged. Just as your personal routines send a signal about what is important in your life, in many ways your leadership routines can serve as a form of coaching as your routines send messages about how it's done.

For example, according to a *Harvard Business Review* article, truly successful companies and their managers know how *not* to waste time. Some of their techniques include "measuring the real value of every time on the agenda." They prioritize items and deal with the tactical issues prior to a meeting, either by phone or e-mail. The pared-down agenda deals only with decisions that have to be made, not discussions about the decisions. Discussions take place before the meeting. (Mankins, 2004)

At one health organization, the CEO stresses that "a leader needs to keep peoples' noses to the grindstone and raise their eyes to the horizon." Keep track of the must-do items while thinking about the long-term impact of decisions. In other words, manage today with an eye toward tomorrow. He also keeps to a strict timetable. Instead of delaying decisions, this leader emphasizes the need to continually ask, "When does this decision need to be made?"

If you made a list of the tasks that are priority items for you today, what are you routinely doing to both make progress on those items and to reinforce their importance? Your list will, of course, be unique to you and your leadership position; however, a manager's typical list might include the following:

- Aligning your team
- Minimizing risk
- Moving priorities forward
- Building internal and external relationships
- Monitoring and tracking team progress
- Building future capability

What types of leadership routines could help with each of these priorities?

DON'T FORGET THE FUN STUFF

Routines at work aren't about just getting work done. Don't forget to create fun routines for celebrating successes (large or small), traditions, or unexpected "moments of delight." Fun routines are as much a signal of what's important as work routines—important enough to celebrate, important enough to become a tradition, and important enough to recognize the moment.

At Duke CE, our Durham offices are located in one wing of a historic building that once housed a tobacco warehouse. Upon entering, the entry level and the floor above are both visible and accessible as there are open stairs and balconies surrounding the high entryway. In the past, whenever there was something important to share, people would walk around trying to gather everyone to this central location to hear the news, and although this was more personal than an e-mail, it was not very efficient. So, we installed a ship's bell in the open stairwell. It is only used for special announcements. It's now become a tradition that when you hear the ship's bell ringing, you know that there is something significant to celebrate. We can listen to the story, get the details, ask questions, and offer congratulations. For anyone who isn't able to join in for whatever reason, their coworkers later deliver the news personally.

IDEO describes itself as a company that helps other companies innovate. They help others with the creative process of designing products, services, environments, and experiences for their own clients. Tom Kelley, general manager of the design firm, describes the unique end-of-project awards that team members design for each other as a way to emphasize the team's accomplishments and celebrate individual contributions. Occasionally, teams create awards that poke fun at themselves by playfully recalling a blunder during the project, such as the studio head who mistakenly submitted a reversed drawing and was later awarded a mirror on a plaque. Other awards celebrate extra effort, for example, a Superman doll lifting a shopping cart over his head to the person who worked almost nonstop to complete a shopping cart design. (Kelley, 2001) Consider creating a recognition system for your own team.

- *Recognize milestones.* Don't wait for the "big" success or final phase of a project in order to celebrate. Recognizing and rewarding the milestones along the way keeps us engaged in the process and send a signal that what we're working on really is important.
- *Reward one another.* Encourage and enable team members to recognize and celebrate their own accomplishments. Recognition from coworkers can be the most meaningful because they are closest to the action and know the full implication of your efforts.
- *Rewards shouldn't be routine.* If rewards are allowed to become *too* routine—given for "standard" effort, given too often, and not indicative of individual contributions—they can actually deter the team's spirit rather than build it.
- *Recharge and renew the spirit.* Encourage people to take small breaks to recharge and renew. Miranda's husband Joseph has a routine each year in March. No matter what else is happening at work or at home, Joseph flies down to Florida with his brother for three days of spring-training baseball. They drive from one small ball park to the next, sitting in the sun and watching a game they love. Joseph returns rejuvenated and relaxed.

RENEWAL AND FLEXIBILITY

Routines should create structure and stability, but shouldn't be stifling or stagnating. We're reminded of a film several years back where a weatherman, Phil, is reluctantly assigned the obligatory February 2nd coverage of the groundhog (or "rat" as he calls it) in Punxsutawney, Pennsylvania, who will supposedly predict six more weeks of winter or an early spring. This is Phil's fourth year on the story, and he makes no effort to hide his frustration. But Phil soon discovers that things are worse than they first seemed, because for him, time has stopped. He finds himself in a time loop, forced to repeat Groundhog Day over and over again. After a few days of repetitive actions—knowing what will happen next and what people are about to say—Phil finally takes it upon himself to mix things up a bit in order to break out of the holding pattern that he finds himself in.

If your own actions start to feel not only routine but dull, habitual, mechanical, or monotonous, then it's definitely time for a change. That doesn't mean you need to toss out everything and opt for complete spontaneity and unpredictability; instead, reassess which routines are actually useful to you. Remember, situations and needs change. The routines that work today for you, your team, your family, or any domain of your life will have a limited life cycle. Recognize when they are no longer working and need to be recalibrated. Even routines that are meant to be enjoyable can become stale if you don't build in some variety or surprises. Pay attention to the clues that others may be giving you when things have started to become *too* routine.

Even more dangerous is when our thinking becomes routine. Sometimes our habits become so ingrained in our thinking that we don't even see them as habits but just "the way things are." Take care that routines don't develop into barriers that reduce your group's creativity. Although they can help with the easy things, you don't want routines to become so ingrained that people no longer think. It's these times that we need an occasional jolt to get us out of our mental patterns. Roger Von Oech (1998) believes that we need this occasional "whack on the side of the head" to stimulate us to think about our world differently, ask new questions, and generate new answers.

At Duke CE, we sometimes use improvisation games to help managers break their routines or broaden their mindset. In one game, participants are forced to think of alternatives to the flow of a story every time someone else says "new choice." For example, a narrative might sound like, "I woke up one morning, surprised to see a new car in my driveway." *"New choice." ". . .* and I scratched my head." *"New choice."* . . . and I grabbed my bicycle." The point is to be able to spontaneously see that there are other options, other possible ways the action can flow. When we tie it back to the participants' real lives, they begin to see that if they shift their own thinking, and begin to say "what if we . . ." they might in fact get better results. It's a small but powerful shift. (We offer a special thank you to our partners at Performance of a Lifetime for working with us on these program segments.)

Lead a More Cosmopolitan Life

This can be an effective way to combat the tendency to drift into too much routine. We don't mean that you should begin booking your tickets and renewing your passport; but simply interacting with others beyond your own area—other teams, divisions, clients, suppliers, and business partners—helps to reduce ruts and introduces a wider array of "fodder" so there is more to draw on when you need to be creative. Going out to community events or the theater, reading a different newspaper or magazine than you normally do, striking up a conversation with someone you've never spoken with, or trying a new kind of food are simple examples—expand your experience and get engaged more broadly.

By connecting, staying in touch, and listening to those beyond your own group, you'll also begin to predict when routines will need to change. Kouzes and Posner (2003) call this using your "outsight," or looking outside your immediate environment for stimulation and information.

Recognize and Take Advantage of Opportunities to Connect

Routines are often about managing time but also involve being opportunistic, and opportunities come in all sizes and at unexpected times. Use them to build and maintain your relationships. It doesn't have to be a lengthy commitment. Small intervals and moments can be just as effective; use the elevator ride, a break during a meeting, or the walk to your car at the end of the day to stay connected to others. Go outside the routine to take advantage of situations and unexpected opportunities. When the unexpected happens, use it as an opportunity to develop creativity rather than as an indication that you need more "policy."

Let's say you've blocked out two hours on your calendar every day for taking care of important items that are frequently overwritten on the calendar. When other demands challenge this time, you may have to decide if this new item truly is an opportunity or instead a diversion. It may be that the new opportunity really is more important. As Marcus Aurelius' *Meditations* note, "Time is like a river made up of the events which happen, and a violent stream; for as soon as a thing has been seen, it is carried away, and another comes in its place, and this will be carried away too."

Make New Opportunities When You Reject Others

We're reminded of a story that one team member told of knocking on the door of her new boss's office to see if he could chat for a few minutes. She rarely initiated one-on-one conversations with him, but wanted to talk about how she was struggling with her current assignment. Her boss told her that his calendar was full, and she should schedule something for later in the week. She didn't ask again and neither did her boss pursue the request. The issue remained unresolved and she eventually resigned. The opportunity to strengthen the existing relationship and perhaps begin a coaching process was there and recognizable, but unfortunately ignored.

Social Invitations Are Also Networking and Learning Opportunities

Gwendolyn disliked parties since she had divorced. So she simply stopped attending parties that were held several times each year by her firm. She particularly dreaded the biannual one-day retreat and had made excuses to skip the last two. She reasoned that these events were for younger employees anyway. She was familiar with the company's mission and didn't need to hear yet another "pep rally" with some outside "guru" hired for the occasion.

But this year, her director changed the retreat's format and added a new and surprising element. Instead of going solo to the day-long Saturday retreat, Gwendolyn's director asked each employee to bring one professional friend from outside the company. That might be fun, Gwendolyn thought. She invited Charles, a documentary film maker from a local university who was a friend from her gym.

At the retreat, each company employee introduced his or her friend, who then talked about his or her work. Questions and answers followed, and the discussions took unusual and unpredictable directions. The retreat had no stated goal, other than "thinking out of the box." The unstructured day turned out to be not only enjoyable, but useful too. People talked about all sorts of ideas, and with the new voices came new perspectives. At the end of the ten-hour day, Gwendolyn felt energized. The old retreat routine had been broken and the result was rejuvenating.

In retrospect, Gwendolyn realized that she actually learned things at that retreat. She heard different ideas that spawned new ways of thinking about old problems. After the retreat, she changed her marketing routine. Instead of just evaluating the work product, she would invite the marketing associates into her office for an hour or so. She let them talk about concepts they had rejected and why, even allowing them to vent a little frustration about the creative process. Why this change?

She remembered one owner of an advertising agency who made this comment at the retreat: "No matter how much time thinking about, worrying about, focusing on, questioning the value of, and evaluating people, it won't be enough," he said. "People are the only thing that matters, and the only thing you should think about, because when that part is right, everything works." (Wademan, 2005)

Gwendolyn gleaned from that retreat more than she expected, but it wasn't factual knowledge that she gained. It was simply to put new routines in place. In addition to listening to her marketing associates, she added more socializing time, including meeting with her associates for lunch every few weeks, and listening to them brainstorm and sort through new accounts. She found that by isolating herself less and getting to know her workers on a more casual basis, they were a more productive team with better quality creative content.

CHECKLIST

❑ Using the Time Management Matrix, outline where you are currently expending the most energy and effort. Is it in the right places? How can some routines help?

❑ Which routines are critical for *you* doing your work versus critical to instill in your direct reports? Why?

❑ What leadership routines are working for you today? Where could you do better?

❑ What are the implications of your choices for others?

CHAPTER FIVE

LEADING THE WAY

IN THIS CHAPTER

Striding on the Runway: The Role Model ■ "I Am the Great and Powerful Oz" ■ Transitions Come in All Sizes

So far, we have discussed the need for a personal vision—a set of guiding values or aspirations that help define what you want—and the need to form some plans around those. We acknowledged that those plans will change as new opportunities present themselves, and how, by using your vision as a basis for decision making, you still can seize those opportunities while remaining true to yourself. We also discussed calibration, the periodic assessments you need to do, the adjustments you need to make, and the milestones you need to celebrate.

In this chapter, we turn our attention outward, to your leadership role and how you affect others. Recall that we argue that to find equilibrium for yourself, you need to keep these guiding principles in mind.

- Be clear about what you value and where you want to go.
- Build and keep strong relationships.

- Approach life as a series of shorter intervals rather than as a marathon.

Now that you have gotten a clearer sense of your values and priorities, it's time to consider the relationships you have.

Your role places you in a unique position to observe, interact with, and influence others. *As a leader, your job is to help people stay focused, provide the right environment, and then turn the people loose to do their thing.* You need to consider what they can do for you, and what you can do for them, all in the service of a set of outcomes. The relationships you have with your people and with others in your network give you leverage. Through those relationships, you can get work done, shape others' behaviors, and help them find equilibrium as well. Remember, life is dynamic and interconnected—by leading your people well, everyone's life can be better.

If you have children, one analogy would be your role as a parent. You, the parent, have to create structure and boundaries for yourself and for your children. They can't do everything (sports, academics, music lessons, time with friends) and they, too, need equilibrium in their lives. You help them get that by *using routines* (bedtimes, dinnertimes, homework times), *having clear priorities* (homework is done before video games are played), *measuring and reinforcing* those priorities (grades, school awards, good sportsmanship), and *modeling behavior* for them that demonstrates your values and preferences (being on time for dinner, coming to their recital or sporting event when you said you would, using appropriate language, putting money into savings accounts). To be successful in your role as a parent, you also have to create your own personal routines, understand yourself and your priorities, create your own definition of parenting success (kids are happy, kids have empathy for others, kids get into college), and find your own equilibrium points. If you are too far out of equilibrium, you'll have difficulty being a good parent or, similarly, being a good leader.

STRIDING ON THE RUNWAY: THE ROLE MODEL

Mohandas K. Gandhi said: "You must be the change you wish to see in the world." One interpretation of this quote is that each of us can be an instrument of change just by living in a way that reflects the world we want to live in. By living in congruence with our values, we can shape the world to better match those values. Especially with leaders, people take note of what you do and say, and they look to you as an example of how *they* should act and what *they* should say. You are a role model for others.

Although professional basketball player Charles Barkley denied being a role model, the truth is that anyone in the public eye *is* a role model. Face it: As a leader, you are in the public eye (albeit a smaller eye than an NBA game audience). As such, you need to make conscious choices about how you behave. You can draw attention to the behavior you want to demonstrate and play down what might distract or contradict. For example, you might view keeping your word as a critical value. If you promised to have some information back to a client by close of business today, instead of taking an afternoon break with your team, you remind them of the promise and excuse yourself. Your behavior models reliability, and that, hopefully, creates a culture of reliability.

The important part is to be consistent in what you say you're going to do and what people observe you do. If you're not, you lose credibility. If you told someone that proper nutrition is important, and admonished him to eat sensibly, you would hope the message makes sense and would be convincing. Now, imagine delivering that message while munching on a large order of french fries and washing them down with a milkshake. How credible are you? Similarly, if you tell your team that submitting their travel expenses on time is critical and then routinely fail to submit your own, the message is negated.

People model what they see and what they hear. In the case of maintaining equilibrium, it isn't effective to tell people to go home at 5 PM if they see you in the office until 6:30 or 7 each night. Instead, you also need to leave at a reasonable time. One executive we spoke with noted that she is very careful to always leave the office before 6 PM, so her people know that it's okay for them to do the same. If she doesn't leave, they don't leave, even if they have nothing pressing to keep them there. So, she makes sure to say goodnight on her way out the door, signaling that they can leave as well. (She just doesn't mention to her team that she works another hour or two from home each night after her kids are in bed.)

Another executive in the same organization decided that he wanted to coach his children's sports teams. He made sure his team of direct reports knew where he was going every Wednesday afternoon—that family was a priority—and that he would check his messages that evening after 9 PM. He had a tough decision, though, about whether to tell his customers. He decided on a case-by-case basis whether to tell them he was out of the office or out coaching soccer. For some, the details would be well received and strengthen his relationship. For others, they would resent that he had the flexibility to coach, and it might damage the relationship.

Part of being a role model, then, is embodying the messages you want to deliver. This also includes deciding how much to show and to whom. Your values and priorities reveal a part of you that may be private, or that are at the core of how you see yourself as a person. In some cases, you need to show some of that—to build trust, to be credible, to help others have the courage to do the same. In other cases, it may not add to your relationship with another person or be appropriate (revealing religious or political views, for example).

"I AM THE GREAT AND POWERFUL OZ"

*"Condense some daily experience into a glowing symbol
and an audience is electrified."*
Ralph Waldo Emerson

A national flag. An Oscar statue. Kneeling in prayer. A police officer's shield. Standing when a judge enters a courtroom. Choosing Lynn to go to the conference instead of Robin. A private office. All of these are symbols or symbolic actions. They all have meaning in a particular setting. For some, like a national flag or an Oscar statue, the meaning is widely shared. For others, like choosing Lynn, the symbolic meaning may be limited to a small set of people. Your team might realize why you made the choice and see it as consistent with the message you have been trying to convey, while others place no particular significance in her selection.

Many organizations have myths and stories that have been told through the years and have become symbolic. Hewlett-Packard employees hear the story about one of the founders taking a chain cutter to a supply cabinet that had been locked shut, and then posting a note saying something like: "At HP, we trust our employees and anyone, anytime should have access to supplies. Creativity isn't bound by a standard workday, and people should have the tools to invent whenever inspiration strikes." Decades later, the story is still part of the company lore and culture.

Ordinary, daily events and activities can be interpreted as symbolic as well. That is especially true for leaders who are the key communicators of symbols and their meaning within the organization. You can't always define what will or will not be symbolic or control what meaning others will see in your actions; however, it is important to recognize the potential power that symbols have. Something as simple as an inside joke can become symbolic and focus people.

Using symbols effectively is a way you can influence and help guide your team. In the 1939 film "The Wizard of Oz," the Wizard strikes a deal with Dorothy and her friends: If they bring back the Wicked Witch's broom, he will grant their requests. In this scene, the petitioners are all scared, timid, and overwhelmed by the setting—a booming voice, smoke and lights, a grand room with huge doors and nowhere for them to sit. It is clear who is in charge. In their second meeting, once Toto the dog has revealed the Wizard as just a man behind a curtain, the conversation becomes a dialogue among relative equals. Although they call him a "humbug," the Wizard still has some symbols in his back pocket and uses their power to help the group. He grants the Scarecrow a degree in Thinkology, and magically the Scarecrow is spouting off mathematical formulas. He gives the Tin Man a heart-shaped watch and the Lion a medal of valor, and each feels proud. The symbols serve to reinforce what each character desired and had exhibited along the journey.

Symbols can influence a small group or the entire organization. For example, imagine that you work for a nonprofit organization targeting the prevention of teen pregnancy. One way the group tracks statistical data is by placing a whiteboard with updated weekly statistics in the front lobby. You and other staff members walk by the board several times a day, blind to the numbers. Although the statistics are improving in your city, the people in the office aren't getting the message. Motivation is lacking because it's hard to see that your group is, in fact, making a difference.

One morning, you walk into the lobby and stop-in place of the whiteboard is a small table on which pink and blue baby booties are lined up. Nineteen pairs of booties in all and a small sign that reads: "In April 2004, nineteen babies were born to teenage mothers. Let's reduce that number in April 2005." The booties serve as a visceral and concrete reminder that those "numbers" are living and breathing infants. Using the symbol of a baby bootie brings the message home-with luck and hard work, you and your cohorts become energized to work to remove as many pairs of booties as possible by month's end.

Now, envision another setting, this time the lobby of a large pharmaceutical company. A series of large black and white photographs hang on a wall. Each photograph depicts a man, woman, or child in an active setting: a woman sails, a man gardens, and a child plays soccer. The photographs show life being lived to its fullest, reminding the workers that enter the building that their "end-users" are not hospitals or clinics, but people. The photos remind employees that the company's success should be measured not just by its stock price, but by the ability of people to live their lives.

Symbols can rally people to an idea or represent a goal. Gandhi used salt to rally his nation and further their quest for independent rule. In 1930, the British had a monopoly on salt in India. Although it occurred naturally along the coast, it was illegal for Indians to harvest this free natural resource; instead, they were forced to buy it from the British. Given the climate, salt was essential for all who wanted to eat. Using the salt tax to symbolize all the injustices to the people of India was an apt choice because everyone (rich and poor) understood its necessity in everyday life. Gandhi wrote to the Viceroy, noting that he believed "this tax to be the most iniquitous of all from the poor man's standpoint." He then led a march to the coastal village of Dandi, spanning 240 miles and 23 days. The march ended at the sea with him and others picking up the sea salt from the shore. He and many others were arrested for breaking the law. The Dandi Salt March marked a turning point; it was only after this event that the British were willing to negotiate with the Indian people. Salt, a most basic necessity, served as a symbol of a nation unduly oppressed (*cf.* the Boston Tea Party of 1773).

Most of us have smaller aims than Gandhi did. Yet we can use the same tools to help focus people on a clear objective. Let's take a look at one of the world's richest men. Ingvar Kamprad, who founded IKEA, has an estimated net worth of $23 billion (Forbes list, 2005), although some publications have pegged it as high as $50 billion. Yet, he flies economy class, stays in modest hotels, takes the subway and public buses when he can, and otherwise drives a ten-year-old Volvo. Why would he do this? To reinforce his company's core values through his own behavior. IKEA is known for well-designed, functional, and inexpensive furniture created for the masses. From the top of the company, the employees live this philosophy.

From your own position within the organization, consider the following:

- How symbols are or could be used to reinforce your vision and values.
- How to replace negative symbols with positive ones.
- How symbolic stories can be used to motivate your people.
- How *you* are used as a symbol.

TRANSITIONS COME IN ALL SIZES

You are well placed to observe others and strongly influence the environment in which your team works, the tasks they do, and the support they get. They are interdependent with you; their ability to get results in the office and find equilibrium in their own lives is partially dependent on their relationship with you, their life at work, and the boundaries they perceive.

We know that people often struggle during major transitions. Major changes in any of our life domains, especially those that have been stable and our "anchors" in the midst of chaos, will affect all aspects of our life. People may work longer hours following a promotion, which means less time for reading the newspaper or professional journals. They may need to spend more time working through child care issues following a divorce, which means absences during "standard business hours." They may be assuming greater financial obligations for aging parents, college tuition, or weddings, which in turn can lead to considering how they can increase their earnings through new roles or career shifts. Such transitions are a large shock to a person's life system and take some time to work through. They have to find new ways to handle the dissonance in their lives, find new stabilizing points if you will, before they can get comfortable again. Given the benefits of successfully navigating these major transitions—to the person, to you, and to the organization—what can you do to help?

Create a Relationship of Trust

It is easier to observe a change if you are already engaged with a person. In our book *Coaching and Feedback for Performance,* we talk about a leader's role in developing talent and in coaching direct reports. Having a coaching relationship allows you to detect any signs of trouble sooner than if you weren't interacting regularly with the person. It also makes it easier to initiate conversations and ask questions because you have already shown that you care, that your intent is benevolent, and that the person can trust you with the answer. It also lets the other person know that it's okay to approach you and ask for your advice or assistance. If you are a coach, it's your job to help, so it's not a weakness for the person to need help, nor is it an intrusion on your time, because this is what your time is for.

Observe and Be Proactive in Recognizing When Others Need Help

You can sometimes anticipate a transition and find ways to help people through it. Some people will be proactive and seek you out. They may want to change some aspect of work, such as their role or their schedule. In such cases, it helps if you are open when they approach you. In other cases, people may not recognize the trouble they're in nor seek out the help they need. They are so overwhelmed that they don't even take the time to stop and realize they are snowed under. They are in survival mode and don't realize they are not functioning effectively. In such cases, you need to observe and then extend an invitation to talk. If you don't have that kind of relationship with the person, then find the appropriate person to initiate the conversation. Either way, be proactive. Be responsive. Be involved. See that they take mini vacations, even if only a day or two, to renew, reflect, and rejuvenate themselves after especially stressful or intensive tasks or events.

Be Creative in Helping Others Consider Options

A direct report approached her supervising manager and asked for a private meeting. She explained that, reluctantly, she had to resign her position. She wanted to return to college. At 33, she had about 21 course-hours left to complete her degree, and if she didn't do it now, she would never do it. Her son was in school, her husband and parents were healthy, and this had to be the time. Her manager listened and asked specific questions: Where would she take classes? Did the school offer online or evening classes? What kind of degree was she seeking to complete? Her manager also asked a lot of questions about the logistical issues of her decision, finally asking the employee whether she would consider working part-time while she studied. It might increase the time it took her to finish her degree, but she also could keep some salary and benefits, and the company would ultimately benefit by holding on to her institutional knowledge and skills. With a willingness to be flexible, a normally destabilizing event was handled with little difficulty.

Recognize and Manage Micro-Transitions

Major transitions across life chapters can cause a disruption in routines and goals; therefore, we're typically more conscious of them. They are also more observable to those around us. In response, we work together to find different support or patterns to our lives. However, we face a series of micro-transitions every day that can be disruptive in their own way. These are the typically recurring transitions that we make each day without thinking much about how smoothly we're making them. They might be transitions from one meeting to the next, from home to a party, from one job to another job, from one task to another task, or from one call to the next. They cause us to quickly shift from one context to another, and make the adjustment in our thoughts or behavior to match what we need to do in that new context. (Ashforth, Kreiner, and Fugate, 2000)

Some people are able to make these shifts easily and smoothly. Others need a break or boundary, something to mark the end of one activity or role and the start of the next. Ashforth, et al. proposed that those who shift smoothly have more integrated roles or identities; that is, there isn't a big difference in the type of roles they play in different settings. Other people have stronger boundaries, and have more segmented roles or identities. Similarly, some people are good at seeing patterns or connections between elements and are flexible thinkers. Others are good at focusing on details, and diving deeply into a topic; it may take them longer to "pull out" and move to a new topic.

Micro-transitions are likely to increase in frequency for most of us. The amount of time we can devote to any conversation or task seems to be shrinking, so as a survival skill, we need to learn to redirect quickly. Consider the talents, capabilities, and personal aspirations of the people you have and the type of work they need to do. How can you help them, and yourself, make micro-transitions? Consider the following suggestions:

- *Observe and reorient as you move from domain to domain, meeting to meeting, or task to task.* Take 60 seconds to ask yourself: What's the objective of the next event? What's involved in the task? How do I engage this person?
- *Consider what activities need a longer block of time and protect it.* Set firm boundaries and say no. For example, if you know that a team meeting agenda contains a number of issues that people feel strongly about, allow more than the standard one hour to allow everyone to speak and still make it through the important items.
- *Be clear at marking end points.* Instead of letting a number of issues float, get good at closure and reducing the number of loose ends. Summarize the progress, decisions, and action items.
- *If you need a break, create one.* Go to the bathroom or get a beverage if you need a moment to clear your head. Observe others and give them a break as well.
- *Work on flexibility.* Make a conscious choice to try a different approach to a common task. Run a meeting in a different format. Let someone else take the lead.

CHECKLIST

❑ Consider your own leadership behaviors:
  - Which are most observable?
  - Which are consistent with the messages you want to convey?
  - Which are not reinforcing those messages?

❏ What symbols or symbolic actions exist today for your team or organization?
  • Which are most observable?
  • Which are reinforcing the messages you want to deliver?
  • Which are not reinforcing those messages?
❏ What can you do to be better prepared for large and small transitions?
  • Who among your people needs assistance today?
  • Who among your people is likely to need assistance in the future?

ALL LIFE IS AN EXPERIMENT

"Don't be too timid and squeamish about your actions. All life is an experiment."
Ralph Waldo Emerson

LIFE IS DYNAMIC

We live in a world that continues to change. The life cycle of technology is getting shorter. The prevalence of personal communication devices is increasing. The distinction between home, office, and elsewhere is blurring. Yet, amid these shifts and others, we need to function and achieve, and we need to do it faster.

In this book, we have explored how you find focus, recalibrate, work through transitions, and rely on others. We've discussed ways you can leverage yourself through others and find your equilibrium points. As you make changes to your lifestyle, to better retain focus and move forward, keep in mind that it's not always easy to do.

- *There will be tension and tradeoffs that you will need to resolve.* Sometimes, there is tension when you have to decide what the most important thing is at this moment: Do you go to your niece's wedding or your best friend's 75th birthday party? Do you keep your scheduled team meeting or use that only available opportunity to meet with a valuable colleague and mentor who is in town for the day? At other times, there is tension within our relationships: Do you move across the country to support your spouse's promotion and give up your job, or do you say no to one boss in order to say yes to the other?

- *There will be change.* As you move between chapters in your personal life, family life, or work life, your equilibrium points will change. Recognize those changes, and that the way you will be most effective will change along with it. As a single person, Jane was able to travel for work as often as needed. She used her weekends to catch up on laundry and bills, and took short vacations to see her family. Then she met Chris. She underwent a transition in how she spent her time—finding a way to travel less, getting laundry done during the week, reading news at the gym instead of listening to music—in order to free up time to spend with Chris.
- Continue to be conscious of your choices, mindful of your priorities and successes, and reflective of your progress.

LIVE A COSMOPOLITAN LIFE

In an earlier chapter, we talked about flexibility and having to be creative in helping people make transitions and find equilibrium for themselves. To be a successful leader, you need to provide input and ideas, to spark people's attention and energy, and be open to different perspectives. By doing so, you can get amazing results.

In a study of Nobel Laureates, a researcher asked what their lives were like at the times they felt the most productive and did their best, most meaningful work, and also at the times they felt least productive and did work that they weren't particularly proud of. The common theme was that they did their best work when they were focused on fewer projects and were leading a varied life. Their least productive periods were marked by too many projects and too many hours spent at work. Being cosmopolitan gave them a leg up. Being cosmopolitan can provide you with the following:

- Gives you a broader range of experience and broadens your perspective.
- Broadens your network of relationships and potential for collaboration.
- Exposes you to new options, and potentially new solutions that you hadn't considered.
- Let's you get creative, to help make the new opportunities work.

YOU ARE NOT ALONE

A theme we have come back to time and again in this book (and in this series) is how important relationships are. Proof positive: A group of scientists studied how women typically respond to stress compared to how men do. Women typically adopt a social response: "Tend and befriend." They create and maintain social networks that help them to reduce threats and feel safer. Men, on the other hand, typically rely on a "fight or flight" response. The researchers conclude that the social support women favor has positive health benefits and "may help to explain the 7½ nonspecific years that women live longer than men." It helps emotionally and practically to have relationships and to draw on the help and support of others. (Taylor, et al., 2000)

You may have heard the expression, "Use your network." That's good advice. Our writing team has used their networks to find jobs, meet spouses, get information on any subject you can think of, borrow equipment, tour factories, meet ministers and heads of state, buy houses, plan weddings, cope with funerals, and create a business that thrills our clients and satisfies their needs.

The point is, you aren't alone, so don't try to do it all yourself. You have social connections, so use them. Continue to look for ways to expand your network, such as the following:

- Volunteer for cross-functional projects that will introduce you to new teams and areas of your company.
- Join a community organization that matches a current interest or talent that you have, or attend an event that you haven't had an interest in previously.
- Invite people to lunch with you. Get away from the office and have conversations.
- Take a class in something new or something that you used to enjoy.
- Call an old colleague or client and renew the connection. You aren't calling because you *want* something, but simply to see how and what they are doing.

Recall also that you should be prepared to help in return. Our writing team has used our own networks to help others apply to graduate school, get jobs, plan weddings, cope with funerals, do research, connect with external resources, and relocate to new cities or even countries. Consider the following in your relationships:

- *How are others doing?* Your domains intersect with others'. Maintain your network of relationships and be observant of others having difficulty maintaining their equilibrium.
- *What can you do to help others?* Explore how the reinforcing and supporting techniques—goals, calibration points, success measures, routines, or simply a mini vacation interval—could help. Are there ways that your unique talents could help them with a particular task?
- *How can others support you?* Their unique talents may be just right for some of the tasks that you don't have a gift for.

There is no magic formula nor is there a recipe for the "perfect life." All we can do is be thoughtful about the opportunities we come across, make conscious choices, and then do our best to be effective when executing those choices. Know what you value. Live each chapter fully. Surround yourself with good people and enjoy the relationships. If you can live in a way that keeps you close to equilibrium, regardless of the choices you make along the way, then you've found your recipe for a great life.

BIBLIOGRAPHY

Ashforth, Blake E., Glen E. Kreiner, and Mel Fugate. 2000. "All in a Day's Work: Boundaries and Micro Role Transitions at Work." *Academy of Management Review* 23: 472–491.

Aurelius, Marcus. *The Meditations of Marcus Aurelius.* Trans. by George Long. Vol. II, Part 3. The Harvard Classics. New York: P.F. Collier & Son, 1909–14; Bartleby.com, 2001. www.bartleby.com/2/3/. (March 21, 2005).

Blanchard, Ken, Bob Nelson, and Stephen Schudlich (Illustrator). 1994. *1001 Ways to Reward Employees.* Workman Publishing Company; 1st edition.

Buckingham, Marcus, and Curt Coffman. 1999. *First, Break All the Rules.* New York: Simon & Schuster.

Buckingham, Marcus, and Donald O. Clifton. 2001. *Now, Discover Your Strengths.* Free Press.

Covey, Stephen R., A. Roger Merrill, and Rebecca R. Merrill. 1994. *First Things First: To Live, to Love, to Learn, to Leave a Legacy.* New York: Fireside.

Covey, Stephen R. 1989. *The Seven Habits of Highly Effective People.* New York: Free Press.

De Graaf, John. 2003. *Take Back Your Time: Fighting Overwork and Time Poverty in America.* San Francisco: Berrett-Koehler Publishers, Inc.

De Waal, Frans B. M. 2005. "How Animals Do Business." *Scientific American* (April): 72–79.

Friedman, Steward D., and Jeffrey H. Greenhaus. 2000. *Work and Family–Allies or Enemies?* New York: Oxford University Press.

Fritz, Robert. 1989. *Path of Least Resistance: Learning to Become the Creative Force in Your Own Life.* New York: Fawcett-Columbine.

Groppel, Jack L., and Bob Andelman. 1999. *The Corporate Athlete: How to Achieve Maximal Performance in Business and Life.* New York: John Wiley & Sons.

James, William (1892/1961). *Psychology: The Briefer Course.* Gordon Allport, ed. New York: Harper & Row.

Kelley, Tom, with Jonathan Littman. 2001. *The Art of Innovation.* New York: A Currency Book.

Kerr, Stephen. 1975. "On the Folly of Rewarding A, While Hoping for B." *The Academy of Management Journal* 18(4): 769–783.

Kofodimos, Joan. 1993. *Balancing Act: How Managers Can Integrate Successful Careers and Fulfilling Personal Lives.* San Francisco: Jossey-Bass, Inc.

Kouzes, Jim, and Barry Z. Posner. 2003. *The Leadership Challenge, Third Edition.* San Francisco: Jossey-Bass, Inc.

Loehr, Jim, and Tony Schwartz. 2003. *The Power of Full Engagement: Managing Energy, Not Time, Is the Key to High Performance and Personal Renewal.* New York: The Free Press.

Maister, David H. 2000. *True Professionalism: The Courage to Care about Your People, Your Clients, and Your Career.* New York: Touchstone.

Mankins, Michael C. 2004. "Stop Wasting Valuable Time," *Harvard Business Review* (September) 58–65.

McCarraher, Lucy, and Lucy Daniels. 2002. *The Book of Balanced Living.* Rollinsford, NH: Spiro Press USA.

McCaskey, Michael B. and E. Mary Lou Balbaky. 1981. *Strike in Space.* Cambridge, MA: Harvard Business School Publishing. Reprint 9-481-008:1–15.

Merrill, A. Roger, and Rebecca R. Merrill. 2003. *Life Matters: Creating a Dynamic Balance of Work, Family, Time, and Money.* New York: FranklinCovey Co.

Paredes, J.A., and M.J. Hepburn. 1976. "The Split-Brain and the Culture-Cognition Paradox." *Current Anthopology.* 17,121–7.

Pink, Daniel H. 1999. "What Happened to Your Parachute?" *Fast-Company* (September) Issue 27: 238.

Quinn, James Brian. 1992. *Intelligent Enterprise.* New York: The Free Press.

Senge, Peter, et al. 1994. *The Fifth Discipline Fieldbook.* New York: A Currency Book.

Taylor, Shelley E., et al. 2000. "Biobehavioral Responses to Stress in Females: Tend-and-Befriend, Not Fight-or-Flight" *Psychological Review* 107(3): 411–429.

Von Oech, Roger. 1998. *A Whack on the Side of the Head.* Third Edition. New York: Warner Books, Inc.

Wademan, Daisy. 2005. "The Best Advice I Ever Got," *Harvard Business Review* (January): 36.

INDEX

Share the message!

Bulk discounts
Discounts start at only 10 copies and range from 30% to 55% off retail price based on quantity.

Custom publishing
Private label a cover with your organization's name and logo. Or, tailor information to your needs with a custom pamphlet that highlights specific chapters.

Ancillaries
Workshop outlines, videos, and other products are available on select titles.

Dynamic speakers
Engaging authors are available to share their expertise and insight at your event.

Call Dearborn Trade Special Sales at 1-800-621-9621, ext. 4444, or e-mail trade@dearborn.com.

Dearborn™
Trade Publishing
A **Kaplan Professional** Company